YACHTING
MONTHLY

Further
Confessions

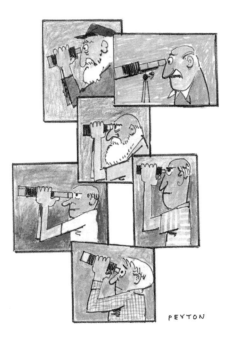

PEYTON

YACHTING
MONTHLY

Further Confessions

Yachtsmen own up to their sailing sins

Edited by Paul Gelder

Cartoons by Mike Peyton

ADLARD COLES NAUTICAL
London

Contents

Preface **vii**
Mike Peyton **viii**

A moving experience • Mark Grimwade **1**
A bird in the ... • Enid Croft **2**
Sex, dives and videotape • David Child **3**
An expert opinion • Mike Gentle **4**
The end of my tether • Peter Thomas **6**
Dry boat • Linda M Corrie **7**
Having read the book • C J Thorp **8**
It's a frame-up • John Lockhart **9**
Rough passage • David Weston **10**
Piled up • Tina Mellenie **10**
Vile vire • Terry Abel **12**
Moondance • Jamie Davies **13**
Unda-estimated • Michael Fraser-Hopewell **14**
Raging inflation • Derek Hyde **14**
It takes two to tango • Charles Stock **16**
Technical know-how • David Newman **17**
Nude awakening • Chris Southwood **18**
Heading for safety • Jerry Green **18**
Whale of a time • Tony Belcher **20**
Instruments never lie – do they? • David Morrison **21**
All eyes • John Newton **22**
Mud larks • Paddy Abbott **24**
It's a flare cop • Jonathan Vander-Molen **25**
To the rescue • Peter Flood **26**
Sight for sore eyes • Hamish Rogers **27**
Lighten our darkness • Malcolm Moore **28**
A birthday to remember • Barry Higgs **29**
Topless Avon lady • John Willis **30**
Pole position • S R Parfitt **31**
Buoys won't be boys • David Palmer **32**
Sinking feeling • Jan Ledochowski **33**

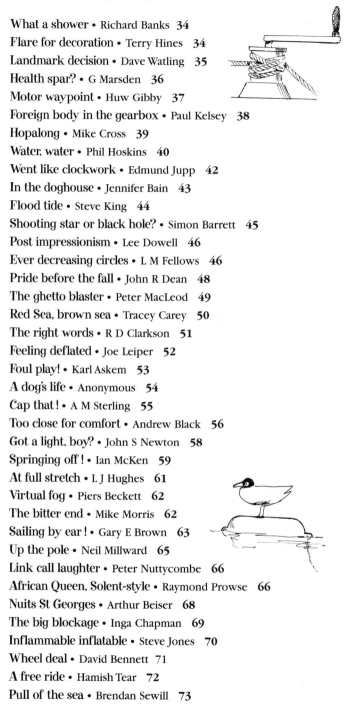

What a shower • Richard Banks 34
Flare for decoration • Terry Hines   34
Landmark decision • Dave Watling   35
Health spar? • G Marsden   36
Motor waypoint • Huw Gibby   37
Foreign body in the gearbox • Paul Kelsey   38
Hopalong • Mike Cross   39
Water, water • Phil Hoskins   40
Went like clockwork • Edmund Jupp   42
In the doghouse • Jennifer Bain   43
Flood tide • Steve King   44
Shooting star or black hole? • Simon Barrett   45
Post impressionism • Lee Dowell   46
Ever decreasing circles • L M Fellows   46
Pride before the fall • John R Dean   48
The ghetto blaster • Peter MacLeod   49
Red Sea, brown sea • Tracey Carey   50
The right words • R D Clarkson   51
Feeling deflated • Joe Leiper   52
Foul play! • Karl Askem   53
A dog's life • Anonymous   54
Cap that! • A M Sterling   55
Too close for comfort • Andrew Black   56
Got a light, boy? • John S Newton   58
Springing off! • Ian McKen   59
At full stretch • L J Hughes   61
Virtual fog • Piers Beckett   62
The bitter end • Mike Morris   62
Sailing by ear! • Gary E Brown   63
Up the pole • Neil Millward   65
Link call laughter • Peter Nuttycombe   66
African Queen, Solent-style • Raymond Prowse   66
Nuits St Georges • Arthur Beiser   68
The big blockage • Inga Chapman   69
Inflammable inflatable • Steve Jones   70
Wheel deal • David Bennett   71
A free ride • Hamish Tear   72
Pull of the sea • Brendan Sewill   73

Anchor buoy dance • Peter Dronfield   74
At the sharp end • Brian S Ferguson   75
Rude awakening • Margaret Smith   76
Jetsam revisited • Ian Hudson   77
Yellow peril • Gordon Cobban   78
Doorstop technique • Robert Cundall   79
Hungry hamster • Amanda Ivey   80
Heads and tales • Jim Abbey   81
Lift and separate • Diana Jung   82
These fuelish things • Deborah Christiansen-Lee   83
Ah, the trials of youth! • Alan Otterburn   84
Laid up legless • Julian Burn   85
Bucket and don't chuck-it • Peter Crowther   86
Creature from the deep • George H Shields   87
Bare-faced cheek • Roger K Steele   88

Published 2002 by Adlard Coles Nautical
an imprint of A & C Black Publishers Ltd
37 Soho Square, London W1D 3QZ
www.adlardcoles.com

Copyright © Yachting Monthly 2002

ISBN 0-7136-6152-6

A CIP catalogue record for this book is available from the British Library.

A & C Black uses paper produced with elemental chlorine-free pulp,
harvested from managed sustainable forests.

Typeset in $10^1/_2/13^1/_2$ Garamond Book
Printed and bound in Great Britain by The Cromwell Press,
Trowbridge, Wiltshire

Preface

Sailing is a great leveller. Faced with a dragging anchor, a stranded or sinking boat or the perils of going aloft, the expertise of any sailor, whether an experienced Yachtmaster or a humble buoy-hopping day sailor, can be tested to the limits. In such situations, a wry sense of humour is often as useful as an RYA certificate.

It was Des Sleightholme's idea to launch The Confessional column in *Yachting Monthly*, back in 1983, a year before he retired as editor. 'Every yachtsman who ever went to sea,' he mused 'has, somewhere, a skeleton hiding in his cupboard, an incident he would rather forget but which still preys upon his conscience.'

How prescient he was. Readers clamoured to 'own up' to their most embarrassing moments. For over 20 years, The Confessional has become one of the first pages that readers turn to each month. We've seen it all: liferafts that turned into death rafts, outboards that fell overboard, leading lights that drove away, bowsprits used in 'jousting matches' – real-life cock-ups stranger than any fiction... and all with the chilling unspoken postscript, 'there but for the grace of God go I'.

In this sequel to the first successful collection of 'the best of The Confessional', a new host of nautical mishaps require you to suspend belief. Experience is the name we give to our mistakes, said Oscar Wilde. But why not learn from the mistakes of others? Why be a sinner when you can be so saintly? Wouldn't it be churlish to ignore such cautionary tales from such selfless confessors? Read on and let incompetence be your instructor afloat.

PAUL GELDER
DEPUTY EDITOR, *YACHTING MONTHLY*

Acknowledgements:
Thanks to Kirk Camrass and Toby Hodges for assistance in research and proof reading.

Mike Peyton

For many years the much sought after prize for those brave enough to publicly confess their sailing sin was an original Peyton cartoon. Mike Peyton, a writer as well as cartoonist, is sometimes known as the Giles of the sailing scene. His keen eye for humour afloat has inspired 17 books of cartoons and some 2000 Confessional cartoons.

Mike has owned 13 boats, from a Folkboat to a Dutch botter, and three ferrocement boats, *Brimstone, Lodestone* and (his latest) *Touchstone*, a 38ft (11.6m) ketch. There is no truth to the rumour that his next boat will be called *Tombstone*.

Mike's cartoons have been published in sailing magazines from Yokohama to Yarmouth. He lives on the East Coast in Fambridge, on the River Crouch, and still draws cartoons for the best Confession each month in *Yachting Monthly*.

Further Confessions

A moving experience

Back in the mid-1950s, I was fortunate – and amazed – to find myself skippering a crew of school and work friends aboard the Bristol Channel Pilot Cutter *Hirta*.

Our midsummer cruise took us first to Ostend. In those days, *Hirta* had a petrol/paraffin (TVO = tractor vaporising oil) Gray engine, with a huge thirst and many other problems. Needing more fuel, the large crew formed up with jerrycans lashed to oars and marched to the nearest filling station.

'Three hundred litres de para-fine, *s'il vous plaît?*' They didn't understand.

'Three hundred litres de tay-vay-oh?' I tried again. Same response.

I knew it wasn't benzine. Impasse. The crew shifted impatiently, mindful of the fact that the bars were opening.

Then an old gentleman who spoke some English came across and asked if he could help. I tried to explain about the paraffin; he suggested we try a shop down a side street and told me to ask for something by a word I didn't recognise and can't now remember.

Off marched the scruffy crocodile to arrive outside a small shop with a window display consisting of some faded papers and innumerable dead flies. On my request for '300 litres of (the word I can't remember)', the owner peered sadly over his glasses at the line of crew bearing jerrycans on oars.

Turning back to me, he asked, 'Monsieur, they are *all* constipated?' • *Mark Grimwade*

A bird in the ...

Picture the scene: it is a warm summer's evening at the Folly Inn, in Cowes, Isle of Wight. We are enjoying a pre-dinner glass of wine with our friends, Derek and Barbara, on their Moody 35. They had motored here two days earlier on glassy seas after attempting to sail from the Hamble. As we sipped our wine and enjoyed the tranquil surroundings, the only slight annoyance was a squeaking noise from the rigging. Derek adjusted the halyards, inspected fenders, and tightened a rope here and there, but the squeak persisted. It seemed to get worse whenever the mainsail cover was touched.

'Sounds like a bird,' I said.

Derek peered into the end of the sail cover.

'My god it is!' he exclaimed. 'There are faces looking at me!'

Inside the sail was a nest with four hungry birds chirping for food. What to do now?

Thoughts of going back to the mooring on the Hamble were

mooted, but would the parents still be around after two days? Derek decided to phone the Royal Society for the Protection of Birds on his mobile phone. We were told there was no RSPB officer on the island. It was suggested that we try the RSPCA instead.

The mobile phone battery was now low, and there were mutterings of 'this is costing a fortune!' before, finally, a friendly voice agreed he could come to investigate.

The twittering of the birds was now loud and urgent. They hadn't been fed for two days. At last, the nest was removed, and the birds identified as pied wagtails. The RSPCA man took them off with a promise of mealworms.

The thought of the sail being hoisted didn't bear thinking about. And the name of Derek's boat? *Magic Flute*! Opera buffs will know that it features the birdcatcher, Papageno. • *Enid Croft*

Sex, dives and videotape

I was in love again. I had first seen her when I was in Mull some 30 years before. She, riding her pony, had disturbed the deer and ruined our day's sport.

Years later, we met again at the funeral of a mutual friend's father, and one thing led to another. I had a spare few days and proposed a sailing trip on the Norfolk Broads. I borrowed a

sailing cruiser and we set off from Horning on a blissful evening, running with wind against tide past all the thatched riverside houses, towards St Benets ruined Abbey. All very Arthur Ransome!

We stopped and moored for the night. We were the only people there. I woke early and went up on deck, leaving my new-found love in her bunk. I hoisted the sails, let go the mooring lines and pushed off. Except I didn't make it back on to the boat, and dived awkwardly into the water.

After a while the sound of flapping sails made it obvious to her that something was not quite right. It was only when she looked up and saw I was not in the cockpit that my strangled cries revealed – I was in the water.

She sprang into action. She leapt on deck stark naked. At which point, the only motor cruiser I had ever seen on the Broads before noon came out of the dyke.

'My friend's fallen in the water,' she called to the boys in the motorboat. That was pretty obvious, and not entirely helpful. Eventually, she managed to tie a bowline round a winch to provide a loop that I could get my foot into.

My friend then realised she had no clothes on, and that the youths on the motor cruiser were videoing the whole thing!

• *David Child*

An expert opinion

It was a lovely bright, breezy day in spring as we sailed down the Exe estuary and skirted Bull Hill Bank on our way to the mouth. The boat was *Lyonesse*, a 6.7m (22ft) lifting keel sailing cruiser – pride and joy of my friend Rob who had built her.

What Rob wanted was my 'expert opinion' on her sailing ability and general seaworthiness. He was also anxious to impress his wife, Sandy, as he was trying to interest her in sailing.

As Exmouth Docks came abeam we realised that it was going to be a dead beat out through the channel to reach the open sea. The tide was ebbing, and we needed a series of short, sharp tacks to get us out between Pole Sands to the west and Exmouth beach to the east.

Rob passed the tiller to me, telling his wife casually that I knew the channel like the back of my hand, and I started to beat out towards the sea, gingerly at first.

After a few crisp tacks we had made quite good progress and Rob and I both began to relax. He started to extol the virtues of his 'baby'.

'This is where the lifting keel is such an advantage,' he declared proudly. 'Even if we do touch on one of the tacks, the keel will simply ride up and we can spin around on to the other tack.'

My confidence was growing. 'We wouldn't even mark the keel,' I said. 'It's all sand here anyway.'

At that very moment *Lyonesse* ran aground. We were stuck fast on what turned out to be an isolated rocky ledge and were all sent sprawling across the cockpit as the keel was lifted to half-raised position. The boat then heeled alarmingly as the current, now running at 4 knots, pushed her over. It wasn't until later that we discovered that the shackle joining the lifting cable to the keel had slid itself sidewards and jammed itself hard into the keel box.

Rob and I jumped on to the ledge and tried to push her off, but to no avail. I decided to try just one more method. With the main halyard in my hand I tried to pull *Lyonesse* over to reduce her draught. As I pulled, I walked backwards on the rocky ledge and, just as she was almost on her beam ends, I took one more step off the edge and into the deep water. The sudden extra weight of me disappearing underwater yanked *Lyonesse* right over and, helped by the strong ebb current, she slipped off the ledge, springing suddenly upright and shooting off down the channel.

I was still holding tightly on to the main halyard at the time and could then be seen hurtling into the mast like some sort of demented Tarzan. As I sailed through the air I began to realise what could happen, but too late. Letting out a yell of dismay, I landed agonisingly on the deck with one leg on either side of the mast!

There was chaos in the cockpit as we drifted astern in the tide, sail trailing in the sea and a very harassed Rob trying to explain to Sandy that this wasn't the norm, and sailing wasn't usually like this.

We motored back to the mooring very quietly – tidying up as we went. The soles of my feet, which had been quite badly cut on the rocky ledge, left funny red patterns on the white deck, and my pride was pretty cut up too. • *Mike Gentle*

The end of my tether

Many years ago we lived in Budleigh Salterton and kept our yacht on a buoy in the Exe Estuary. One summer I brought our 2.4m (8ft) GRP pram dinghy to Salterton beach, intending to fish for mackerel just offshore. I went down in the evening to launch and as usual there was a surf running on the pebbly beach. I gave the dinghy a shove, but before I could grab the oars we broached and were thrown back on the pebbles. I tried a second and third time, whereupon the dinghy capsized on top of me and I crawled up the beach like a turtle looking to lay its eggs.

By now a small but appreciative crowd had gathered. Red with embarrassment, I righted the dinghy and gave a most prodigious push. We got through the surf and I grabbed the oars with a sense of achievement. The only trouble was that when we capsized, the dinghy anchor had fallen out and was now on the beach at the end of its warp. My one consolation was that a Salterton fisherman, who in those days used 3.4m (11ft) clinker-built dinghies which could carry their way through the surf, was laughing so much that he too broached, thus adding to the entertainment. • *Peter Thomas*

Dry boat

'Ingress of water' has become a family catch phrase, inspired by my husband's obsession for keeping our various boats dry. His crusade, however, took on greater significance when fitting out *Serin*, our Wing 25. Holes drilled through the hull are real anathema to him, and to minimise these (and because of financial restraints) we fitted a flushing-type chemical toilet instead of a marine loo.

On launch day, *Serin* was lowered gently into her natural element, and friends and boatyard men toasted her with something suitable. Such was his phobia about the dreaded ingress, however, that Robert was headfirst in the engine compartment all the while, checking the sterngland and seacocks for leaks, of which there were none.

In the nine years of sailing since, *Serin*'s bilges have remained absolutely dry of salt water. The only trouble in the early days was caused by our inability to make the hatch in the cockpit floor totally watertight against real deluges of rain. With the help of a cockpit tent when she is left on her mooring, we seem to have cured that problem.

Since then it has been customary to taste any residual water found in the sump to confirm that it is rainwater or accumulated condensation, and to satisfy ourselves of the integrity of hull inlets.

Then, on one famous occasion, Robert dipped his finger in the few inches in the bottom of the bilge, tasted it and triumphantly pronounced it 'definitely not salt', but then, somewhat dubiously, 'not very fresh either'. The fluid was duly mopped out.

Shortly after that, we discovered the two halves of the chemical toilet had not been sealed together properly at its last emptying.

Recently we installed a marine loo. • *Linda M Corrie*

Having read the book

I knew nothing of the sport of sailing but, having 'read the book', was full of misplaced confidence. After patching and painting my new acquisition, a heavy old marine ply catamaran, I towed her to Torquay Harbour, where I stepped the mast, launched her, and hoisted the sails. I wasn't sure about the fold-up rudders, so I tied them in the up position.

A strong offshore breeze was blowing as my girlfriend and I cast off from the safety of the slip in the outer harbour. I had to explain that sailing did not mean sunbathing on a sailing boat, and asked her to help me fend off moored boats until we reached the main fairway.

I got us aimed down the fairway at the gap in the harbour wall, sheeted in both sails, and tied them off with landlubber knots. Then everything started to happen faster than the book had led me to believe. We accelerated to an incredible speed, heeled over at an alarming angle, and my girlfriend was engulfed in a plume of spray, down on the leeward float.

I shouted down to her to climb up, but she froze and clung on for dear life. I couldn't help her, because I needed both hands and all my strength on the tiller bar to stop us rounding up into the moored boats skimming past our windward side.

I had no choice but to try to hold course through the harbour entrance but, just as we approached the gap, it seemed to close, with a large passenger ferry entering. Now I had a choice: hit the ferry or the harbour wall at full speed.

At that moment the mast snapped, and the sails almost immediately scooped up water and stopped us, like an aircraft landing on an aircraft carrier.

Suddenly all seemed silent. The ferry glided into her berth, as if nothing had happened. But I was hooked on sailing. I needed a new mast fast, and a new girlfriend. She never went sailing again. • *C J Thorp*

It's a frame-up

A couple of years ago I was spending the summer living on my Oyster 39 in the South of Spain. In a small marina, one hot, sunny day, I was asked by the au pair of a well-to-do family if I would take them all sailing. They would bring the food and drink and we would sail slowly along the local coast.

Shortly before they were due to arrive, there was an accident down below. Shouting Catch! to my friend, I threw him a heavy object; he missed and it hit the louvred heads door. One by one, in slow motion, all the louvres fell to the floor like a pack of cards, leaving only the empty frame.

We picked up the louvre slats, started the engine and cruised out of the harbour. Shortly after, while I was fixing a drink in the galley, one of our four guests asked if she could use the loo.

'Certainly,' I replied, indicating it opposite the galley. She entered and pulled the now empty door frame closed behind her. I continued fixing the drinks and it was not till I went to take the drinks on deck that I realised she was sitting in full glory, quite unaware and unconcerned about the missing louvres. She subsequently opened the door frame and appeared on deck to tell her companions where the loo was and how to use it.

In cold panic I wondered whether to tell her, or say nothing, and we spent the rest of the day with the ladies either oblivious to the situation or else thinking that the English yachtsmen were a little odd.

They never came back for another day's sail. • *John Lockhart*

Rough passage

The inn sign of The Bugle was held nearly horizontal by the bitterly cold blast, aided and abetted by generous helpings of sleet and snow. Joe and I shot like corks from champagne bottles through the door into the snug bar, where we ordered half pints of bitter. Even in 1962, our apprentices' salaries of £115 a year did not allow for anything more stimulating.

As we began to thaw out we discussed our voyage up from Lisbon. The Bay of Biscay had lived up to its reputation, with the mad March gale pursuing us all the way around Ushant and up the Channel, never dropping below force 10.

There had been mayhem out at sea, with extensive damage across England. Trees and chimneys had been toppled and the umbrellas of city gents turned inside out.

Imagine our delight when the landlord came over bearing pints and whisky chasers 'courtesy of the yachting gentlemen at the bar'. They had overheard our conversation and were proud to stand us a few drinks. A few more rounds arrived and we became tolerably happy, even perhaps a little confused.

We never did get around to telling them that we had not made the trip on a yacht. Our 16,000 ton tanker had come through remarkably well and was discharging ballast at the refinery just down the road at Fawley. • *David Weston*

Piled up

The boat was a very elderly 40-footer with a hazardous 6ft bowsprit. We were motoring up the Beaulieu River, intending to tie up between two trots and go ashore for a civilised lunch.

'You go forward and grab the ring, and I'll put her as close as possible,' commanded the skipper. Alas, however close he got to the pile, I couldn't get a line through the ring.

'You take the helm and I'll tie her up!' was his alternative plan.

Gingerly, I took the helm – I was still rather new to this – and edged cautiously up to the wooden pile. The skipper balanced precariously on the end of the bowsprit to grab it. As the bowsprit approached ever closer to the pile, I lost my nerve and went into reverse. Unfortunately, the skipper had already committed himself and had his arms around the pile. He had a desperate decision to make as the boat moved astern and he chose the relative security of the pile.

I was left alone at the helm, reversing down the river, paralysed at the sight of him clinging with arms and legs around the slimy wooden pile!

Eventually, I went ahead again and motored gently past him, not capable of speech, although he made up for that deficiency!

I carried on up the river, wondering what to do. Somehow I turned around before it got too shallow and came back down. Yes, he was still there. Fortunately, by this time a local ferry man had stopped laughing and taken pity and came out in a dinghy to rescue him and return him to the yacht. I shall draw a veil over the next few minutes.

Although we are no longer together (not, I hasten to add, because of that incident), I can still see him in my mind's eye clinging to that pile! • *Tina Mellenie*

Vile vire

It sat there throbbing and gurgling in the engine bay, like a contented baby, doing what comes naturally, slurping water up the intake pipe and spewing it out in satisfying smoky gushes through the transom. Could this be the same old rusty lump that I had exhumed from the bowels of my Z 4-tonner? Had it really burst back to life at the first turn of the key after my ham-fisted attention? I couldn't believe my eyes, my ears or my luck.

I strutted around the pontoons, grinning with idiotic pleasure and accosted fellow berth holders with a cheery wave and a grin, anxious to share my good news. They mumbled encouraging things like 'Oh, it works then!' before remembering something urgent to attend to below, or at home, or anywhere.

The tide ebbed away out of the Blackwater and it was time to let the oystercatcher's plaintive call replace the steady throb of my trusty Vire 12. Silence reigned and life on the stagings returned to normal. In the next berth, Tim whistled softly as he painted the giant winch on his foredeck bright yellow. I put the kettle on. It was then that I remembered I hadn't tried the gearbox. But in that crystal moment I knew that the prop would only be half-submerged in the soft ooze. If I kept the water intake shut, I could run the engine for a few moments just to check the propeller actually turned.

My trembling hand turned the ignition key and the engine burst instantly to life. I eased the gearshift

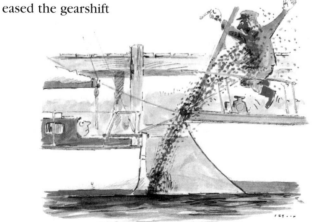

forward and (oooh, deep joy) the shaft began to revolve. Then, above the roar of the engine, another sound rose, like the bellowing of a wounded beast.

A furtive glance from the companionway revealed a skyline familiar to everyone who has watched muck-spreaders at work. My eye followed the trajectory of the mud, and on Tim's once pristine foredeck an animated oozy mass was jumping up and down, waving a paintbrush dementedly. I just caught the last strains of the bellowing, 'IT STILL @*+ING WORKS THEN!'

• *Terry Abel*

Moondance

Coming up the River Severn in *Daisy*, our motorsailer, Sue and I arrived just too late for Diglis Lock, so we dropped back and moored in shallow water away from the channel. In the early hours of the morning we were both woken by a persistent 'pinging' sound.

'It's a rat!' whispered Sue. 'Nonsense, it's just the hurricane lamp swinging against the shrouds,' I said reassuringly. But soon I had to admit that while swinging lamps ping, they certainly don't scrabble and make gnawing noises. So I dressed and went into the wheelhouse to investigate. The brilliant light of a full moon flooded in through the windows, and I saw a small mouse chewing at our steering cables. I tried to catch it, but was too slow.

Then Sue had a go. Moments later there came the cry of 'Got it!' She was dangling the mouse by its tail, but as it tried to arch upwards and bite, she started to jig about wildly and the creature began emitting high-pitched 'eeks'. Sue climbed on deck and continued to jig about as I shone a torch on the riverbank looking for a place to deposit the creature.

Across the river two fishermen stared with open mouths. Only then did it sink in that my wife was wearing absolutely nothing. The anglers had watched a beautiful young woman dance naked beneath a full moon to the feverish rhythm of unworldly eeking noises! • *Jamie Davies*

Unda-estimated

We'd just bought a second-hand Nauticat 44, and the original owner wanted to take the name with him to his new boat. 'What a wonderful opportunity,' we thought. 'For the first time we can actually name a boat ourselves rather than be stuck with someone else's inevitably inappropriate choice.'

Funnily enough, it wasn't easy, but eventually we came up with what we thought to be a brilliant name, *Unda*, which is Latin for wave (as in undulate). Nauticats are built in Finland, and I had worked closely with a Finnish company called Unda a few years before – work which provided part of the wherewithal to buy the boat. What more appropriate and clever name could you think of?

Off went the form to Swansea, with the three choices you are required to submit. *Unda* first, with a second choice of *Amicus* and *Tartan Tramp* thrown in as a desperate attempt to come up with a third. Back came the notification that we had been allocated *Tartan Tramp*.

After letters of appeal, and many pleading phone calls to Swansea, they finally relented, and we were allowed our first choice. With the brand new lettering proudly stuck on the stern, and beautifully hand-carved teak placards with the new name, plus a wave motif, on each side of the wheelhouse, we proudly set off on our maiden voyage, a delivery trip from Emsworth to Cornwall.

'I'll just notify the Coastguard of our passage and ETA,' I told my wife. 'Solent Coastguard, Solent Coastguard, this is yacht *Unda*, yacht *Unda*. Over!'

You can still occasionally hear us on the VHF, instantly recognisable when I identify us as 'Yacht Uniform, November, Delta, Alpha. Over.' • *Michael Fraser-Hopewell*

Raging inflation

Having bought his boat and rectified the surveyor's reported defects, the proud new owner was determined to have a sail before the approaching winter.

Undeterred by the prospect of rain, he put the liferaft on the afterdeck, motored out of Sutton Harbour Marina, hoisted sail in Plymouth Sound, cut the engine and relished his new love.

Predictably it rained... and rained and rained. Water cascaded off the mainsail like a waterfall, into the cockpit, and down the drains.

Eventually the rain stopped and autumn sun emerged. However, it was about to return. Just off Mount Batten the engine was started, and the sails dropped. Off Fisher's Nose the engine began to make strange noises and sputtered to a halt. Almost instantaneously there was a bang aft and the liferaft started to inflate, its growing bulk invading the cockpit. The tiller was beyond reach and then the engine stopped. Anglers on the quay, treated to a rare and entertaining sight, gave sarcastic shouts of encouragement.

During the sail, the unattached liferaft lanyard had found its way down through the cockpit drains, swept there, no doubt, by the rainwater coursing through. The lanyard trailed astern harmlessly until the propeller turned. The rest, as they say, is history. • *Derek Hyde*

PEYTON

It takes two to tango

While I admit that many beginners can get in a bit of a muddle, it takes a lot of experience to create a unique muddle and two experienced chaps can always do better than one veteran sailor on his own.

In fact, I didn't need to go into Southwold at all as I was bound for Blakeney, but it looked so attractive in the spring sunshine. The tide was flooding against me on the coast and I fancied a good fry-up for a leisurely lunch.

In those days, 1973, there was a line of mooring buoys down the middle of the narrow harbour, which is merely the mouth of the River Blyth. It was Easter Saturday and most were empty so early in the season. All I had to do was pick up one with my 'grabbit' boathook, which I use from the cockpit when singlehanded.

It is not quite as easy as it sounds, for the tide runs in fast here. As the first buoy raced towards me, I furled the headsail, lifted the centreboard and went for the ring. Missed! Out jib, down plate ready for the next one. I furled the jib but had no time to lift the plate. Got it! I was slow pushing the rudder over as the line tightened and she swung the wrong way. My little gaff cutter, *Shoal Waters*, ended up moored by the bows by a line which passed under the hull *behind* the centreboard and was

thus held beam-on to the current. She responded by swinging back and forth across the river like a wild thing.

By the time I'd stowed the sails, the Cruising Association boatman was alongside to help out. He tried to use the bow of his little clinker motorboat to push the bows of my craft round over the line against the tide. He ended up with the line between his rudder and his transom. The two craft struggled in an embrace that was almost indecent!

Fortunately there was no one to hand with a camera.

• *Charles Stock*

Technical know-how

It was a glorious summer's morning and we had dropped the mooring at Leigh at the top of the tide, perfect timing for our trip to northern France for our holidays. The brand new Perkins engine, just installed by the local yard, started first time.

After only a few minutes, however, it coughed and spluttered, then stopped. Having given it a cursory look I decided it would be best to get the engineer to have a look.

So, after reinflating the dinghy, getting back ashore, making a longish walk to a phone, I waited a couple of hours for the engineer to turn up. Meanwhile, we missed two precious hours of ebb!

On his arrival, the engineer slung his tool box on to the floor of the rubber dinghy, puncturing it - wet feet for the rest of the week - but our valuable ebb took us swiftly out to where our trusty sea dog, *Earl of Essex*, was anchored.

I demanded an explanation as to why the new engine that they had installed didn't work. The engineer, after a quick glance, suggested that we turn on the fuel and see what difference that made.

He didn't need to say more. His expression said it all. A look of: 'And this is the man what's taking his family to furrin parts! Gawd 'elp 'em all.' • *David Newman*

Nude awakening

At anchor early on a summer's morning in Alcudia Bay, Mallorca, the sun was already promising another furnace-hot day. I was alone on my Nauticat 521, *Jazzmin*. Rising from my cabin, I was soon on deck. I sat dreamily contemplating the warm, gin-clear water. Fifteen seconds later I was over the side. A couple of circuits around my boat then to the transom to board, refreshed and happy, ready for breakfast. Except that the bathing ladder was firmly locked in the upright position, out of reach, with the retaining catch two metres above my head!

I tried climbing the anchor chain, but this exited through the bowsprit, which was too wide to pull myself around. Apart from the peril of my silly situation, I came to an even more awful realisation – I was completely naked.

My options: swim to the shore. The harbour was about half-a-mile away, but swimming to the harbourside and emerging from the water naked amongst the patrons of the pavement cafés was not a realistic option. The alternative, which I chose, was to swim to the nearest boat that looked inhabited and knock on the hull.

The freshly woken couple appeared on deck – the water now embarrassingly clear.

'Please, can you take me back to my boat in your dinghy – and may I have a towel?' I meekly requested.

It wouldn't have been so bad if they hadn't looked at each other and then fallen about laughing. Worse still, they were from the same marina. Ten minutes after my 'rescue', I was seen feverishly hacksawing the offending catch on the ladder and replacing it with a metre of shockcord. • *Chris Southwood*

Heading for safety

Seven people assembled in the saloon of my Moody 38, *Lady Livvy*. They were an assortment of business clients invited for a day's sailing. As I went through my customary crew briefing, demonstrating how to use lifejackets, heads etc, two of the seven stood out from the rest: Garry, who was young, had a great sense of humour and had been out on the boat before, and Keith, who was older, had no sense of humour whatsoever and had never sailed in his life.

After my briefing, Garry asked rather pointedly if he could take the crew on deck for a safety briefing. Minutes later I arrived to find the entire crew intently watching Keith, who was sitting with the bright red conical anchor drogue from the lifebelt perched on his head.

A deadpan Garry explained to me: 'I've stressed to everyone the importance, if they fall overboard, of immediately putting on the red conical safety hat attached to the lifebelt that will be thrown to them so they are visible in the wave troughs. I was just checking the crew's head sizes, so we know whether to throw the port lifebelt (large safety hat size), or starboard-side lifebelt (small).' Amazingly, the entire six novice crew members fell for the practical joke.

And my personal need for the Confessional, when it wasn't me that played the joke? It's for forgiveness for the other 22 people who have fallen for it since! • *Jerry Green*

Whale of a time

After a long, lazy lunch in the mess, the skipper tapped out his pipe and asked, 'Who's for a sail in the whaler?' Three stalwart, non-sailing officers volunteered, collected a coolbox of Bulgarian red liquid and the team set off.

Alongside the jetty, in the Army's only maritime unit, they boarded the whaler. The skipper began organising. Mention of halyards, sheets, warps and yards merely served to confuse the crew, but with a 'secure that!', 'pull this!' and 'look lively!', up went the gaff, on went the engine, glasses were charged and the day looked rosy.

The harbourmaster dozed on the jetty, while the NCOs of the landing craft crew alongside mused rightly about the capability of the officer crew. 'Let go!' said the skipper. The senior officer let loose the halyard at the same time as the junior member cast off the lines. The gaff crashed down across the mate and the coolbox, the skipper lost his balance, fell on to the gear lever and the whaler surged forward.

Once the port shroud had become hooked on to the ramp of the landing craft, it became a contest between the whaler's engine and the strength of the shroud. Both being equal, the mast broke and fell overboard. The landing craft crew recognised a cock-up in the making and sensibly retired below.

At that stage, the flares fell into the engine exhaust box, the VHF into the bilges and the coolbox on its side. The leisurely sail now became not so much an accident as an exercise in career survival and avoidance of the CO's wrath. Mast and rigging were cut away, the whaler tidied and a chastened crew went on a tour of the Itchen under engine without further incident. Some hours later the crew arrived safely back.

The coolbox was now empty.

On a scheduled refit two months later, engineers found the flares melted in a dangerous state and welded to the exhaust outlet. An explosive disposal team kindly removed them before further incident. Explosive restrictions on the port were subsequently reconsidered.

The mast was replaced by the ever-helpful RN Dockyard maties at a cost of four bottles of malt.

The last serving officer of the crew retired in September, so the tale can only now be told. I was the skipper. • *Tony Belcher*

Instruments never lie – do they?

We were sitting on Jim's boat in Island Harbour Marina, up the Medina River, musing about the deteriorating weather for the return home to Chichester the next day. For days it had been blowing hard, always from the west. So the return would be fine, being a 'downhill' run, probably under a bit of genoa only.

'Looks like a north-easterly,' said Jim sagely.

Incredulous, I exclaimed that no way could there be any east in the wind, given the forecasts we had been religiously tracking all week. 'Well, that's north,' said Jim, pointing at the ship's compass, 'and the wind's north-easterly.' The compass north was pointing doggedly towards the lock gates. 'But that can't be – there's Fawley chimney, where it's always been and that's more or less north from here – the lock gates are due west!'

'Well, I have confidence in the compass,' said Jim, an experienced sailor with a well-proven boat. 'I'll get the hand-bearing compass.'

Sure enough, the second compass agreed, within a few degrees, with the binnacle. 'That can't be,' said Jim's wife. 'There's Fawley and that's north isn't it?' But who will believe the crew with common sense when two reliable compasses testify otherwise?

A third compass was dusted off – the old RDF set – and unbelievably it also agreed with the other two. I wandered up the pontoon to my own boat, moodily reluctant to believe what I had seen but, nevertheless, lost for an answer. Determined to get to the bottom of this, I checked the chimney with my own hand-bearing compass from my own boat. North! What's going on?

I marched triumphantly back with the news, but still pondering on how three compasses could be wrong. Just before boarding Jim's boat, I took a bearing from the pontoon. East? Now what?

Then, watching the bearing, it shifted 180° as I walked past the huge steel pontoon pile. According to the proximity to the pile, you could make the compass read what you liked!

• *David Morrison*

All eyes

Early this season, I was on a mooring at Cargreen on the River Tamar. The weather was grim but I had to get ashore and, because my outboard was in pieces, I set off to row the couple of hundred yards to the Spaniard's Inn.

At the first, necessarily vigorous stroke, my port oar broke and away I went, drifting down the river. I threw over my little folding anchor to slow the drift, and then stood up and raised and lowered my arms in the prescribed manner.

Half an hour later, the police patrol boat appeared and hauled me back upstream to my original destination. Sighs of relief. End of drama and I was not even wet. I was a bit surprised, though, to be met on the beach by a salty-looking old codger, not known to me.

'I saw you were in trouble and rang the Coastguard,' he said, with an admonitory tone. I grovelled suitably.

'Useless things those,' he said, pointing to my one good and one broken oar.

I could only agree with him and disentangle myself from his disapproval as politely as possible. I set off to the phone box, only to find my path blocked by another, friendlier guy, sheltering under a golf umbrella. 'You must be the chap who was in trouble in the dinghy,' he said. 'I rang the Coastguard about you.'

'Thank you very much,' I said, feeling increasingly embarrassed. I continued on to the phone, made my call, walked to the car park and discovered that I had left my keys on the boat.

PEYTON

Fortunately, I have a friend who lives in the village, so off I plodded to his house to borrow his outboard.

'Hello, heard about you,' he said as he opened the door. 'Someone rang to tell me about you.'

Walking down the village street with him a little later, carrying the outboard, we met a friend of his.

'Ah, heard about you,' he said, after the introductions. 'You must be the guy who got into trouble in the dinghy.'

A bit further down the street the same thing happened. By this time, all I wanted was a hole to crawl into.

What I had not taken into account is that Cargreen is a very popular retirement village for yachtsmen. Many of the houses are new and most are built to take advantage of the view across the river. In many of these rooms with a view, a pair of binoculars is at hand and some even have a telescope on a tripod. A lot of the sailing residents belong to the Cargreen Yacht Club and, of course, they all have phones.

I don't know how many rang the Coastguard – at least four and probably more. Although acutely embarrassed, I could hardly complain, could I? I'm a bit apprehensive, though, about my next visit to the Spaniard's Inn. • *John Newton*

Mud larks

When the tide ebbs from Faversham Creek it leaves from a deep, narrow trench of black, clinging mud. Soon after dipping my toes into the treacherous world of keel boat sailing, I set myself up for a stratospheric jump on the learning curve.

Our Albin Vega was facing upstream and, consequently, we would need most of high water to turn around in the narrow confines of the creek. The owners of Iron Wharf had thoughtfully driven iron spikes into the dyke opposite to enable them to turn their Thames barge around so, I thought, a couple of hours before high water I would take a line across and back to save time.

From my viewpoint across the creek, it looked possible to reach one of the spikes by driving the inflatable flat out and up the remaining couple of metres of mud, even though the bank at that point was on a slope of about 30°. The Seagull outboard was of uncertain vintage but, as ever, thoroughly reliable. The plan was that, as I hit the mud on the other side, the dinghy would ride up the slippery slope and I would kill the outboard and grab the spike.

I set off, armed with a great deal of optimism and several metres of warp. The Seagull was going as fast as it could and my kamikaze approach scattered terrified sheep on the bank.

It didn't work – for two reasons. One, I was a few centimetres short of the spike, and two, the Seagull refused to stop. It dug itself a hole in the mud and, like a demented egg whisk, threw a blanket of stinking black mess in all directions, covering me and the inflatable until we both looked like a lost patrol of an SAS night attack.

The ever-present vultures, gleefully awaiting the unfolding of any maritime cock-up, collapsed in uncontrollable laughter. I managed to stop the engine and, with all the dignity that I could possibly muster, poled the dinghy back into the water. I could not have been more embarrassed if I had bumped into the vicar at the bottle bank. • *Paddy Abbott*

It's a flare cop

On a recent visit to my mother's house in north-west London, I discovered a box containing an assortment of distress flares with an expiry date of 1984. Judging by the state of the box, they had been in the loft of an outbuilding for a long time.

I phoned West Hendon Police Station and was told that any police station could accept them. I asked if my local station would need prior warning and was assured they wouldn't, so I took the flares there.

On arrival, I was asked to enter a small office. I placed the box on the floor, by my feet, and stood behind the high counter. The duty officer asked me how he could help. I told him that West Hendon had said that I could bring my out-of-date flares in for disposal. He looked surprised and asked me to wait. Then I heard him on the phone to West Hendon, saying: 'OK, who's the joker who's sent this chap round here with these flares?'

During an involved conversation he appeared around a screen, phone in hand, and again asked me about my request for disposal. I gave him the same information, adding that on the East Coast one can hand them into the Coastguard and, in fact, some chandlers.

He finally got off the phone muttering about never having been asked to accept them before. I wasn't surprised. Hendon is hardly a yachting centre. He finally asked to see the flares. As soon as I opened the dusty cardboard box, revealing its contents, he roared with laughter and perhaps a little embarrassment.

He confessed that when I'd first entered the office, talking about my 'out-of-date flares', he'd glanced downwards and thought I was talking about my trousers.

It took the further involvement of an inspector, a phone call to the bomb squad and some paperwork before I left the flares with them, some 45 minutes after I had arrived. But it was worth every minute. The duty officer has asked to remain anonymous.

• *Jonathan Vander-Molen*

To the rescue

Carol said, 'Do you think he's alright?' The boat she'd been watching was motionless; no sails set, no engine, no anchor, no crew, no sound. Nothing.

Carol was sailing *Holy Smoke*, our Westerly Pentland, to Brixham when, on a hot, sunny, seamless day, the wind gave a yawn and died three miles from Dartmouth.

'We'd better have a look at them. Engine on! Starboard 10!' I said in crisp, authoritative tones. It was clear what had happened. Some terrible fever had gripped them. Or perhaps fear of solitude had caused them to leap overboard. Conceivably they had run out of water and were lying parched... Perchance one of them had gone mad armed with a cutlass. Poor devils!

I was considering how to deal with the honours showered upon me for my 'rescue' attempt. Most I would decline with a modest smile. Then there was the salvage money.

'I can't see anyone,' said Carol as we neared the boat. It was not until we came alongside, stopped the engine and peered over the sprayhood that the scene before us confirmed our worst fears. Lying prone in the cockpit was the motionless body of a young man. Mercilessly the sun battered down.

'Er,' I said, never at a loss for words. And with that the corpse opened an eye.

'Are you all right, old chap?' I asked.

The thought of his sobbing, grateful wife, on her knees, clutching my strong-but-gentle hand passed through my mind.

'Fine,' he said, removing a pair of headphones, and then, pointing to the radio, near a long, tinkling, liquid-filled glass, explained with a wry smile: 'Test Match.' • *Peter Flood*

Sight for sore eyes

Once clear of the moorings, Jo, an attractive blonde, whom at one stage I had designs upon, was keen to helm. Overestimating her experience, I left *Beluga*, a 7m (23ft) Hunter Duette, in her hands as we sailed out of Chichester Harbour on our first weekend away together. Before reaching the Bar Beacon and heading towards the Solent, I nipped below to check everything was in order.

Concerned that we might collide with an oncoming boat, Jo called me on deck. As I stuck my head out of the hatchway, a motorboat roared past, her wake causing *Beluga* to gybe. The mainsheet snapped across the side of my face, propelling my glasses into the briny.

Jo's confidence was shot to pieces by the confusion. I failed to reassure her when I confessed that I had forgotten to bring my spare pair of glasses and could see no further than the end of my nose. We had little option but to return to the mooring.

Jo felt unable to helm, but I struck upon the idea of using binoculars as replacement glasses. The arrangement worked like a dream. I helmed while Jo pointed out approaching boats that I might not have seen. When it came to picking up the mooring, Jo was dispatched forward with the boathook. Unable to judge distances accurately through binoculars, it took a number of attempts to pick up the buoy.

It was at this point I realised, with Jo up forward at the bow in shorts that, from the expressions of passing crew, I may have seemed to be paying rather more attention than was gentlemanly to Jo's aft through a pair of 7x50s. • *Hamish Rogers*

Lighten our darkness

In a 'fitting out' issue of *Yachting Monthly*, there was this marvellous idea for a combination padlock to secure the boat. At a stroke, no more hassle, no issuing of keys to shoregoing crew, nor hiding them under the equivalent of the doormat, the gas bottle.

The lock worked out quite as well as predicted, until our Rival Owners' Association held a rally at Brandy Hole on the River Crouch.

Our hosts at the Brandy Hole Yacht Club provided deep moorings and a launch to ferry us to and from their excellent clubhouse and bar.

At about 1800, before the river dried out, we had smartened up, twirled the padlock combinations to foil wrongdoers and were ferried ashore to a most convivial evening. The windspeeds of our exploits increased in direct proportion to the ethanol consumed, whilst we sat watching the sun sink over the river.

With the closing of the bar came the call to be ferried back. Full of *bonhomie* and booze, we arrived 'home' and waved farewell to our friends and the launch. Turning to the lock, and with reactions undoubtedly a little slowed by several pints, we came to the conclusion that (a) neither of us could read Braille and (b) we had not eaten enough carrots to see in the dark!

Fortunately, we were not the last to return to our boat and by much shouting caught the boatman's attention before he sped off to a well-earned bed. By the guttering flame of his cigarette lighter, we dialled our number and made it to our bunk. A little torch now lives permanently in the cockpit locker to prevent dreams from becoming nightmares. • *Malcolm Moore*

A birthday to remember

Our previous sortie up the difficult Rivers Ore and Alde to Snape had been spoilt by frequent grounding, due to a faulty depth sounder, and too many guests on board our Westerly Konsort Duo, *Dasby*. This time, it would be different.

It was late August, and my wife and I were alone and planning an overnight stay and a concert at Snape Maltings to celebrate my birthday. We arrived on time, around high water, and were advised to put the inflatable between the boat and the quay so that we would dry out more or less level and not on the slope next to the wall.

The evening was windless. We had long fore and aft lines and springs ready for the falling tide, but all were slack, so we departed for the concert with not a care. At the interval – and to be truthful, feeling rather superior – we decided we would saunter back to the yacht for the quicker and cheaper bar service.

We got back to a disaster. The slightest of breezes had picked up but was sufficient to have pivoted the boat and swung the bow in to the quay. As the tide had fallen, the pulpit had hooked itself over one of the quay-wall stanchions and the boat was now hanging with the bow almost out of the water.

I startled the concert-goers, who were promenading with their drinks, by shouting at the top of my voice for 'Strong men, now!'

The response was instant and each man

that could grabbed a piece of the pulpit and, on command, lifted the boat off and threw it towards the mud. It worked. The only damage was a wire that was rubbed bare. But I was in no state for the second half of the concert, especially after rather too many calming G&Ts. • *Barry Higgs*

Topless Avon lady

We were moored in Gorey Harbour, Jersey, and settled down for a pleasant night, our Avon inflatable dinghy lying astern.

Waking next morning, just as the incoming tide reached the bottom of the boat, my wife and I looked astern. No dinghy! Peering over the side, we saw the Avon sticking jauntily up from beneath the bottom of the boat. A quick tug confirmed that she was well and truly stuck. I am not known for being slow to act, but while I stood momentarily dumbfounded, my wife seized the initiative and plunged over the side, followed shortly afterwards by the skipper, dressed only in Y-fronts.

The water was only up to our knees, and it seemed we stood a chance as we tugged and pushed, but the Avon refused to budge. Even deflating the sterntube with the only valve within reach didn't help. By now the water was past our waists and my wife was topless, having removed her sodden T-shirt. Shivering, we clambered back aboard to be met by a horrified teenage daughter, who fled to her cabin, only emerging when certain that modesty once again prevailed.

Neither she nor her brother were impressed when informed that we would have an eight-hour wait before going ashore. We were stranded!

Later that day our toilet ceased to function. Peering over the side, the reason became all too clear. The Avon was full of the contents of our previous endeavours, and our frantic pumping had created a tight embrace between Avon and inlet pipe. Still, we had a bucket. I swear I saw the glint of binoculars from the harbourmaster's office during our endeavours and wonder what his log entry reads. • *John Willis*

Pole position

We couldn't see the boat from the pub but, sitting outside with a glass of beer, having spent the day scrubbing and antifouling her, we basked in the smugness of a job well done, knowing that she would be afloat and ready to return to our berth in about 20 minutes.

We'd come into harbour on the flood, tied up to the wall, watched the tide retreat, and worked in company with the crew of a bilge-keeler parked in the centre. It had all gone swimmingly... almost as if it were planned.

Back on board, we watched a 40-footer (12.2m) leave, and felt confident that there was now sufficient water to back out and motor the short distance to our berth. I started the engine, the mate cast off, and we were off.

Suddenly, we stopped...I increased the revs...nothing. I said, 'We can't be aground.' The depth sounder was showing just over 3m and we only draw half that.

Thinking of all the work we'd just done on her bottom, I put her in neutral, and we leapt forward, toward the rock shelf that lurked just beneath the surface.

Baffled, I threw the engine into reverse and, with rising panic and absolutely no understanding, realised that we were slipping

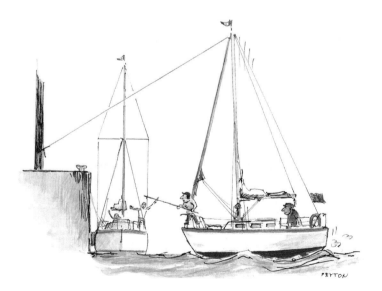

to starboard and describing some kind of arc, with the harbour wall steady on the bow.

With my voice rising in direct proportion to my panic, I brushed aside my wife's questions and told her to get forward with the boathook and prepare to fend off. Our friends in the bilger-keeler watched with puzzlement.

So there we were, in reverse, swinging to starboard and ever closer to the shelf, or, in neutral, shooting forward straight towards it. I had absolutely no idea, except perhaps that we were somehow pivoting around the keel.

No idea, that is, until, looking back in desperation, I saw our friends gesticulating and pointing at our masthead – which was still securely fastened, by the main halyard, to a telegraph pole.

• *S R Parfitt*

Buoys won't be boys

I was on board *Hope and Glory*, a Sigma 36 belonging to Britannia Sailing School, and halfway through my Coastal Skipper practical course. We had left Yarmouth, heading towards Portsmouth. It was a bright, crisp, late autumn day with hazy sunshine.

After entering Portsmouth the skipper decided that with the remaining daylight we should press on to Port Solent at the top of the harbour. With a fair wind, we ran up and dusk fell. Time passed and in the half-light I was struggling to pick out the marks and lit buoys. I had just reached the prime of my life, having passed 40 the previous year, and in the pub that night I decided that I must go and see an optician to get my eyes sorted.

Getting back to the office on Monday morning, I duly made the appointment for that afternoon, turned up and had my vision thoroughly checked.

After the examination the optician said that my vision needed correction and asked me: 'What made you think you needed glasses?'

I replied, without thinking: 'I'm having trouble picking up buoys after dark.' • *David Palmer*

Sinking feeling

Joanna insisted that we get a half-tide mooring in Thorney Channel, Chichester Harbour, at least half-a-mile from the nearest landing point at Prinsted. For access we needed a smart red inflatable dinghy, a bright white Johnson outboard, and all-new warm waterproof clothing. We decided to put it all to the test by motoring out to check our new mooring at high tide, after lunch, one February.

The outboard failed the test an hour after high tide and I started rowing back to Prinsted. But with the ebb outpacing me, we slid backwards. I grabbed a passing buoy and tied up as darkness fell. An hour later we settled on the mud. A northerly wind started blowing from the shore, which was, by now, covered in frost.

We faced an uncomfortable night and I began thinking of ways of escape. After a while I spied a patch of grass-covered bank and got out of the boat to head for it. My first foot immediately sank to the ankle. The next leg sank to the knee. I was then waist deep. I decided to maximise my surface area to the mud by lowering my belly on to it and scrambling back to the dinghy on all fours. Joanne pulled me – and my covering of black mud – back into the dinghy. Black people in a black boat on black mud in a black world lit only by the stars, we held hands lovingly and sang to keep up our spirits.

Many hours passed before we heard the ripple of the returning tide. Then we heard the dipping of oars in the water and saw a shadow row up to one of the markers and tie up. A human form got out of the boat, stood on the mud and did not sink. After a moment of open-mouthed admiration, I said 'Hello'.

My voice, out of the dark, surprised the person, but luckily he didn't lose his balance. He was a fisherman who normally rowed his tender to this point at half-tide and knew a route over hard ground all the way to the shore. He helped us bridge the gap between our soft mud and his spot of hard ground and kindly helped us to lug ourselves, our outboard, dinghy and accompanying mud all the way along his route to the shore.

We gratefully drove home and washed the mud off ourselves in the loos of a Little Chef. • *Jan Ledochowski*

What a shower

Some years ago, after the death of my father-in-law, we were clearing his shed when I found a flat hose rolled up on a reel. It was ideal for the boat, I thought, and I stowed it away in one of the lockers.

Last year we visited Calais in company with friends. While we were both rafted up alongside another yacht, we decided it might be prudent to fill up with water before leaving. In Calais there are no hoses provided, so I thought this would be a great opportunity to use the one I'd been carrying around for the last year.

I dashed below, grabbed it, and passed it over to my friend, who unrolled it and connected it to the tap while I opened my deck filler and inserted the nozzle. 'Turn on!' I shouted, and suddenly we and the boats were soaked in water.

I hadn't realised that the hose was a garden sprinkler – it had holes every few inches along its length.

• *Richard Banks*

Flare for decoration

I write to ease the conscience of my sailing companion, Robin, and as a warning to others on the misuse of flares. He and his wife had just moved into a charming cottage-style house and spent a lot of time and money decorating and refitting it. To their dismay, they discovered a wasp's nest in the living room chimney.

'Smoke them out,' was the advice from work (the local agricultural college), but it was a gas fire.

'Buy a smoke cone specially to get rid of unwanted wasps,' the college pest expert advised.

Rob was never one to waste money. He came from the garage clutching a red smoke flare, the sort used by yachtsmen. It seemed to suit the purpose. After sealing round the fireplace with large quantities of card and tape, Rob pulled the ring on the flare, placed it in the fireplace and then sealed it up with more tape.

All went well, with smoke erupting from the chimney outside. The telephone rang and Rob answered it. I went out to find that smoke was no longer coming from the chimney. Hearing shouting from the living room, I went back in to find red smoke seeping through the cracks around the fireplace and beginning to fill the room. Rob was in a panic, running round opening windows. Flares give off a red powder, not smoke. By the time the flare had stopped, the whole room was covered by a fine red dust, impervious to anything but elbow grease, hot water and detergent. By 0300 we got to bed, leaving a slight pink tinge to the wallpaper, and Rob with a severe ear-bashing from his long-suffering wife. The wasps? Oh, they were fine! • *Terry Hines*

Landmark decision

I was instructing a Coastal Skipper's course during the summer a couple of seasons ago. It was one of those two weeks with little or no wind. We had already spent two and a half days bumping, grinding, warping, and hoisting storm sails and I was trying to think of ways to keep boredom at bay; motoring up and down the Solent was fast becoming mundane.

We had carried out various pilotage exercises earlier, so I thought I'd let a student plan and execute another one without me hanging over his shoulder.

I asked a student to blind pilot our way from Cowes to Hillhead Haven, instructing him that, once we were on the 5m contour, he could pilot the yacht in from the cockpit.

We arrived off Hillhead Haven half an hour before HWS. The student slowed the revs down so we were just making headway and lined himself up for the approach. For those who have never been to (or heard of) Hillhead, the channel markers consist of two beacons with a cross as a topmark.

As we approached, the student missed the first mark and continued heading north up the beach. When I asked him why he hadn't altered course, he replied he could see the port and starboard entry buoys. I racked my memory, had a mental picture of the chart in my head and couldn't remember any lateral marks, so I asked him to point them out.

As he did so, I realised he had observed the green cylindrical wastepaper bin and the red square lifebuoy holder in the car park behind the sailing club.

Throughout this excitement, the shallow alarm had been bleeping and the sounder was showing shallower and shallower. Just before touching bottom, he extracted himself with the gearbox in reverse, spotted the correct mark, and in we went.

• *Dave Watling*

Health spar?

In the middle of Yorkshire, about as far away from the sea as possible, we completed the hull of a 38ft (11.6m) Van de Stadt Seal yacht. After fitting out we launched by crane into the River Calder and moored alongside one of the converted barges tied to the bank.

The engine trials proved successful and we then began assembling a 46ft long mast from a Sailspar kit. After reeving halyards, fitting standing rigging, spreaders etc, the whole unit was stowed on deck. It doesn't take a mathematician to realise that there must have been about 8ft of mast protruding over the bow.

One pleasant summer evening, having shown our rigging work to friends, we motored a few miles downstream to the first lock on the Aire and Calder canal, then turned round and motored back to our mooring, against wind and current.

There were a number of other boats moored and it was a tricky operation. We overshot our mooring, unfortunately striking a barge, which we had intended laying alongside, with our protruding mast. We did not, however, strike the steel topsides or the steel coachroof, but one of the windows. And the window we selected was not the saloon or galley, but the heads where, as Sod's Law would have it, the barge's owner, a rather rotund gentleman, was soaking happily in his bath as 6ft of mast entered his private domain.

As he is a good friend and quite a character, he took it very well. News spread fast along the river bank, with the name of our boat being altered from *RhumRunner* to *RamRaider*. We subsequently repaired the damaged window.

• *G Marsden*

Motor waypoint

This was my first adventure in my own boat – sailing my Achilles 24 from Bristol to Milford Haven for the 1991 Tall Ships Week. My crew had so much confidence in my navigation that he had smuggled a Dinghy Decca aboard.

As it got dark off Port Talbot, we consulted the almanac for the lights of the buoys leading to Swansea: three green lights in line. We soon spotted them, but we were still off the steelworks and the Decca was showing eight miles to go. I remembered reading about Decca inaccuracies at dusk, so we decided to ignore it and follow the lights.

We entered a river to find the lights standing on a training wall. Wharves and cranes were silhouetted on our starboard side. Motoring on, we saw a small marina, yacht club and moorings to port. I had been to Swansea before but nothing rang any bells at all, and it began to dawn on me that we might be lost. This thought was confirmed when the dark outline of a road bridge, towering high above us, came into view. However, it was only after we had passed under the bridge and read the directions on a large blue illuminated sign that I realised we had sailed under the M4 motorway and that we were indeed eight miles from our destination. We had sailed up the River Neath by mistake.

Feeling rather foolish and very tired, we motored back to the club moorings and went to sleep. My embarrassment was not entirely over. At 0400, I was awoken by bright sunshine streaming through the window, and looked out to discover that we were high and dry on the bank of the river.

• *Huw Gibby*

Foreign body in the gearbox

Isle of Aran was a 11m (36ft) twin diesel Thornycroft, built in 1936. She was taking Sue and me and our three young boys to the Mediterranean for a year's cruise.

We had left the Thames and crossed the Channel to Calais with no problems, and were in the canals approaching Douai, when the engine suddenly shuddered to a halt with a seized gearbox. Having no luck in fixing the problem myself, I called in help from the local boatyard. Roger, a mechanic, spent three days stripping the gearbox and repairing the fault. Edward, our seven-year-old, was his biggest fan and spent each day with Roger, 'helping' him.

'I want to be a engine fixer when I grow up!' he told us. From that day on he took a great deal of interest in the maintenance work I carried out.

I kept a close eye on the starboard gearbox and was checking the oil level one day, when I had to go to the bosun's locker to get a new can of oil. When I returned, Edward asked: 'Would Lego hurt the gearbox?'

Not thinking that a small piece of plastic hitting a cast iron housing would matter, I replied 'No.'

Next time I checked the oil level it seemed to be a strange red colour.

'That will be the Lego,' announced Edward. While I was getting the can of oil, Jo-Jo, our youngest, had been feeding Lego bricks into the filler hole!

Although I changed the oil, it still had a faint red colour to it, so I can reliably inform you that a Rimula X and Lego mix will lubricate a gearbox for hundreds of hours. We proved it as we went on to and around the Mediterranean and then back to England. • *Paul Kelsey*

Hopalong

I think I shouted 'emergency stations!' when the jolt woke me. I left my quarterberth like a rocket and in a moment was on the quay looking down at *Sula Sula* straining at her warps. On grounding at half tide, the boat had tipped outwards and was now hanging perilously over the fast-disappearing River Yealm.

Vancouver 27s are built to withstand all sorts of idiotic

handling, but this wasn't good news. I shouted to my crew, Omar, to keep absolutely still and inspected the warps, now taut as railway lines. Everything looked secure, but I didn't like the idea of leaving the yacht hanging like this. Gingerly, I slackened the tightest warp. Then the next and the next. With an awful groaning of ropes around bollards, *Sula Sula* slipped into the mud on her side. No damage done.

Only one problem: how to get back on board? I was standing on a dark quay, barefoot, in the early hours of an October morning wearing nothing but underpants. Time for my crew to earn his keep.

'Omar! Throw me my boots!'

Omar has many talents, but wellie-throwing isn't one of them. After a long wait, a shape shot out of the cockpit, spun in mid-air, and splashed into the mud.

'Omar! Throw the next boot a bit harder!'

This one made it to the quay. I put it on, hopped one-legged down a slipway and through the mud to retrieve my first boot before boarding *Sula Sula* over the stern. Omar was sobbing with laughter.

At dawn we floated off. I tightened the warps and discovered what had gone wrong. As usual when drying out alongside, I'd taken the main halyard ashore to tilt us inwards. It was still there, shackled securely to a ring, but I'd forgotten to make the inboard end fast.

Something to do with the pub opening, I think. • *Mike Cross*

Water, water

We had joined the spacious 45-footer (13.7m) as crew in Antigua. A catamaran, she was fitted with every conceivable extra, including a watermaker that could have supplied enough fresh water to douse the Great Fire of London.

We thought we would top up the tanks, so switched on the generator, which supplied the power for the watermaker, and brought the desalination system up to pressure. Within minutes fresh water was gurgling into the empty tanks.

It would take some time to replenish our reserves, and also fill plastic bottles for the fridge. This was done by thrusting the feed hose from the watermaker leading to the top of the tank directly into the bottles – primitive but easy.

Meanwhile, I went ashore with the skipper in the tender, leaving the generator running. The skipper's wife was in the heads, unaware that she was now alone aboard.

Naturally, we spent too much time ashore and, yes, we had a refreshing drink in one of the local bars. It was some hours later when we motored back through the anchorage. There, waiting in the stern, was our anguished one-woman reception committee.

The generator was no longer generating, so the watermaker was no longer making water. The cause of her anguish was soon apparent. In lines all around the saloon, like a gathering army, were plastic bottles and every other conceivable type of container capable of holding water, filled to the brim. We stood in stunned silence as tears rolled down her face. In a blind panic she had thrown the 'off' switch on the generator, which she thought would cause thousands of pounds' worth of damage.

Our skipper explained in an embarrassed whisper that he had never shown his wife how to shut down the watermaker. Luckily, no damage had been done, but the incident highlights the need for everyone to know how a yacht's system works. In this case, just turning on the tap would have worked. • *Phil Hoskins*

Went like clockwork

The old clock tower has been there for many years, displaying the time to those of us out on the water in the estuary. The structure had been showing signs of its age recently, and work was under way to put right some of the defects.

I had decided to put down some kind of mooring on the beach for the tender and found a suitable spot not far from the tower. I planned to bury an anchor in the soft sand and shingle and run a light chain to a small buoy.

I dug a large hole in the beach and put a decent-sized fisherman's anchor deep below the surface. Then I consulted the village harbourmaster, who advised putting a hefty weight on top of the anchor to make all secure. He said that he knew where there was a suitable weight and went off to find it.

He came back, dragging a great lump of cast iron, and together we managed to dump it on top of the anchor. We tamped down the sand and shingle on top of it, making all secure. Nothing showed but the upper end of the chain from the anchor.

Next morning I strolled down to check all was well. The tide had come and gone, and all seemed in good order.

Then one of the workmen on the tower came over and we chatted for a while. He asked casually if I'd seen anyone hanging about the previous evening.

'Some light-fingered blighter's made off with one of our clock weights!' he fumed. • *Edmund Jupp*

In the doghouse

I had decided to visit my new yacht after my daughter and her friend had spent the weekend on board. I took my two dogs for company – Henry, a very large labrador, and Ronnie, a small Norfolk terrier.

The problem started when Henry launched himself down the rather steep companionway steps with Ronnie in hot pursuit. I busied myself cleaning the loo and cooker, which looked as if an army had been in residence for a week, rather than two teenagers for a weekend.

It was hot so I decided to eat my sandwiches on deck, where there was a nice cool breeze. Henry tried to ascend the companionway ladder and gave up. No amount of coaxing would get him to try to negotiate the upward exit. I wondered how on earth I was going to get seven stone of dog from down below to up top.

A tasty oatmeal biscuit got Henry out of his corner by the cooker but no further. After a re-think I piled two bunk cushions from the aft cabin under the open hatch. I even showed him how to do it by launching myself skyward, but Henry wasn't playing!

Half an hour later, Henry was still most uncooperative and lay wedged against the cooker as I tried my next brainwave. I rummaged in the cockpit locker and found a couple of mooring lines and proceeded to make his car harness into a doggy version of a bosun's chair. Six knots later we were ready.

I slung the long end of the mooring line over the boom and proceeded to winch him up. He got stuck at about the third step up, but he was high enough for me to squeeze past him. A quick heave from behind and we both landed on the cockpit sole in a heap. Henry, none the worse from his unconventional exit, made a dash for the sandwich crumbs while I pondered on the thought that large dogs were definitely not in the equation when my beautiful Najad yacht was designed. Sadly, in future, the dogs will have to stay at home! • *Jennifer Bain*

Flood tide

Yachtsman familiar with St Quay Portrieux will also be aware of the excellent purpose-built facilities at the marina. This has not always been the case. Before the new buildings appeared there was just a large temporary structure with two showers, toilets and several washbasins.

We'd had an exhilarating cruise down from Portrieux, arriving in good time for a hot shower. Under the stream of hot water, I must have lost track of time, which is where it all went horribly wrong.

I didn't notice the lid from a previous user's gel bottle on the shelf, or see it fall on to the floor and block the drain hole.

Eventually, when I'd finished, I was standing in a few inches of water, and so was everyone else. The entire toilet block was flooded, the water from the shower tray having cascaded throughout the building.

It had overflowed through the main door into the car park, causing much amusement for passers-by.

Stepping from the cubicle, I was greeted by a line of faces covered in shaving foam and with murder in their eyes as they sloshed around.

In a sad, feeble attempt to disguise my nationality I tried to mutter something that might have sounded German, before beating a hasty retreat. • *Steve King*

Shooting star or black hole?

For many years I've scanned the Confessional looking for one story from a yachtsman who has never owned up to his heinous crime. So let me tell it here, from the other side of the Confessional box.

In the early 1980s I was a young officer of the watch on a Royal Navy minesweeper patrolling the South Coast. Late one evening we were heading across Mounts Bay to anchor off Newlyn for the night. Although visibility was good there was no moon.

I was alone on the bridge, looking forward to anchoring and a few hours in my pit. I placed a fix on the chart (a visual in those days), ran on my estimated position, had a good look in the radar, and a 360° sweep with the binoculars.

Satisfied all was well, I hopped into the captain's chair and looked at the shore lights about eight miles away. To my amazement, just above the town, I saw a low shooting star arc lazily in the sky. Even more amazingly, it stopped and retraced its path! After a second's incomprehension, I shouted down the voicepipe 'starboard 35!' and leapt out on to the port bridge wing.

I turned on the high-powered Aldis lamp just in time to illuminate a small yacht bobbing past to port, a smiling face giving a cheerful wave. As he fell astern, and I questioned my lookout abilities, all his navigation lights went off and he vanished into the night.

The captain, whose dinner had landed on him during my somewhat violent manoeuvre, was not easily convinced of the yacht's existence.

A couple of weeks later in Falmouth I recognised the errant yacht. The skipper told me that to save his batteries, he never sailed with his navigation lights on, unless he was about to be run down. • *Simon Barrett*

Post impressionism

I recently took my new Bénéteau Oceanis 411 from Bénodet, in south Brittany, to Lagos, in the Algarve. I recruited a crew of three, all unknown to me, to assist with the delivery.

I arrived in Bénodet two days ahead of the crew to install a Navtex and generally prepare the boat for sea. Now, Bénodet is a quiet and unassuming Brittany port, but it also has its 'Blackpool' side, and it was whilst I was exploring this part of town that I had my 'evil', but harmless, idea.

My eye was caught by some postcards of scantily clad bathing beauties. I bought three and sent them to my wife.

On the first, I wrote the message: 'The crew didn't show, so I had to settle for her!'

The second contained only the words: 'And her!' And the third: 'And, alas, her!' I posted them all together from Bénodet.

But for some reason postcards two and three arrived two days before number one.

I called my wife after crossing Biscay and received a very frosty response, to say the least.

'What do these cards mean?' she asked.

'Just a joke, dear,' I replied, not realising she hadn't received the first card.

My wife was not amused and my loving call to say we had arrived in La Coruña safely melted away somewhat. Two days later I received a call from my wife. 'I see the joke now!' she exclaimed.

The first card had finally arrived.

I have now been allowed back into the marital bed, but I sense a virtual lee cloth between us, even now! • *Lee Dowell*

Ever decreasing circles

It was a glorious day for a sail. My yacht, *Kes*, is a 10.4m (34ft) Van de Stadt Kesterloo cutter-rigged steel yawl. Singlehanded, as usual, I slipped my pontoon mooring in Hartlepool Marina and headed for the seaward lock, which I entered in textbook style.

Luckily, *Kes* was the only vessel in the lock as I put her into reverse alongside the pontoon to kick the stern in.

As I stepped off, with my lines ready, all hell broke loose. *Kes* accelerated ahead while I tried in vain to secure her with a line on a cleat. I succeeded only in being dragged along the pontoon on my knees, taking all the skin off my left hand. A 13 stone man can't hold an accelerating five ton yacht. I was either going to end up in the water, or worse, so I let her go.

Kes proceeded to circumnavigate the 15 metre (49 ft) wide lock, passing me at her best cruising speed of about 6 knots. She was too far away to jump on and I was still in slight shock. On her seventh lap, she was getting closer to the north wall of the lock. Would she continue going until she ran out of fuel? A quick calculation estimated that she would run out in two to three days, if she didn't smash herself to pieces on the stone wall first.

She was starting her eighth lap when a chap I didn't know from Adam leapt off the north wall on to *Kes*'s roller-reefed foresail, slid down on to the deck and rushed to the cockpit to stop the engine. He steered her round the circuit once more to lose way and then she glided up to the pontoon to stop without a scratch on her gleaming black hull.

The gear cable on the engine's Morse control had come adrift, giving me only forward gear but increasing the revs when I thought it was in neutral. Since that nightmare, I always enter any lock with extreme caution. • *L M Fellows*

Pride before the fall

Westhaven Marina, in Auckland, New Zealand, had only swinging moorings in the 1960s. At the time, my wife and I were living on board our 10.4m (34ft) Seagoer yawl. One day, while my wife was at work, I put the boat alongside piles to scrub the bottom and antifoul between tides. As the tide came in and she floated and I reversed from the piles, I allowed myself a moment of pride at my independence and sailing skills.

Raising the gaff mainsail and shutting down the engine, I eased out the mainsail and left the sheet slack so that we were broad reaching at about one knot. Going forward, I had the jib about halfway up when there was a gust of wind with a change of direction, and the mainsail gybed all standing. As the main came across, the mainsheet caught up one of the quarter cleats, putting the boat on a close reach and picking up speed straight for a gin palace with so much glass that it looked like the United Nations building.

There I was on the foredeck with the jib halfway up thinking: Should I hoist the jib quickly and hope she will pay off enough

to miss disaster? Or should I take a couple of quick turns on the halyard and try to get back to the cockpit and release the mainsail?

I decided on the latter, wondering how I was going to pay for the damage that seemed inevitable. Insurance was a rarity in those days.

Clearing the mainsheet and turning the wheel downwind, she started to pay off and I thought we were going to make it. Then the end of the bowsprit hooked up on one of those magnificent windows and my yawl came to rest impaled on the result of my ego.

Since that time, whenever manoeuvring in close quarters, I have always made sure that sails were ready to hoist, the anchor ready to let go, and the motor kept running until clear.

• *John R Dean*

The ghetto blaster

I was aboard a friend's yacht for a shakedown first trip from Oban to Tobermory on the west coast of Scotland. After an excellent meal at anchor in Tobermory Bay, we savoured our drams as darkness fell.

'Let's try the stereo,' someone suggested. Stereo speakers seemed ideal for listening to our favourite Scottish music.

The sound proved disappointingly faint, so we turned it to full volume and enjoyed an hour of entertainment. What we did not realise was that there were two further speakers in the cockpit, and the output switch was directing the music to them – at full volume.

It suddenly dawned on us that neighbouring yachts were flashing spotlights and sounding fog horns in our direction.

On climbing up into the cockpit, we realised we were ghetto-blasting the entire anchorage at midnight with reels and jigs.

As a conservative, retired bank manager with impeccably good manners, both afloat and ashore, I cut the stereo, extinguished all lights and we crept out of the harbour at an early hour. • *Peter MacLeod*

Red Sea, brown sea

Before leaving Cyprus for the Red Sea, we invited some friends aboard for a farewell drink.

That afternoon, the holding tank, which we had forgotten to empty after a recent cruise to Turkey, began to smell. It wasn't too bad and we'd be sitting in the cockpit anyway. Some air freshener. No, a lot of air freshener. By 1700 hours the stink was atrocious.

Suddenly, my partner, Larry, decided to give the pump a few strokes. I wondered what this would achieve when the same horrific thought struck us both. We scrambled into the cockpit to witness a seething river of three-week-old excrement flowing down the sidedeck.

A few days earlier we had thought we could minimise potential smells by removing the deck cap for ventilation.

Well, what to do now? Our guests were due at 1900. Panic. The only option was to empty the tank. Engine on and full throttle out of the marina entrance with **** everywhere and sun awnings flapping wildly.

Larry set to removing the sun covers when plop went his left shoe. I couldn't turn until the awning was fully down, so the shoe was soon out of sight. Finally, after tacking back frantically, I sighted it, but it was sinking! The boathook was useless, so Larry leapt into the dinghy and rowed like mad. Rescue successful, we resumed our mission.

Two miles out, the clandestine pumping began, but the excitement was not over. Looking behind me I noticed that our dinghy cover was gone. Off we went again, zig-zagging back the way we had come.

Eventually, I spied a bubble of fabric slowly giving in to the downward pull. Larry sprinted off in the dinghy again. After a second rescue we pumped like mad. Then Larry dashed about clearing up the evidence of our drama as I returned to our berth.

It was 1845 hours. We had a quick rinse, put on some decent clothes and when our guests arrived we were relaxing in the cockpit with a couple of cold beers, one wet shoe, a soggy dinghy cover and no poo! • *Tracey Carey*

The right words

Two weeks into our Christmas cruise and heading north from New Zealand's Hauraki Gulf, we were seeking shelter from the increasing north-easterly wind. By 1700 our 11m (36ft) ketch was tucked nicely into Mimiwhangata Bay.

Forecasting force 7–8, we had placed our anchor with some care, and now lay-to a 36 lb Danforth which pulled well into the sand and mud bottom. Rosemary was feeling a little uneasy as *Te Rapunga* danced and sprang at the warp and, knowing that we could be in for a rough night, suggested we lower the huge fisherman pick we generally keep for emergencies.

'If it's going to give you peace of mind, I don't mind setting it.'

So I proceeded to shackle up. By this time, night had fallen and a vicious wind was gusting out of the bay.

The following morning, wind dropping, we prepared to weigh anchor. My surprise was complete when, on looking over the bow, I saw the line of the chain hanging straight down into the sea. The anchor fluke was neatly hooked over the bobstay, where it had hung all night.

Red-faced, looking around furtively, but with no other boat in sight, I was chuckling merrily when I arrived back at the cockpit.

'Did you have a good sleep, dear?' I enquired.

'A beauty, what a difference it made putting out the big anchor.'

I couldn't contain myself and laughed heartily, much to her puzzlement, until I confessed. • *R D Clarkson*

Feeling deflated

I kept my Newbridge Coromandel *Athena* on a swinging mooring in Findhorn Bay. Before launching her for the new season, I motored out in my Avon rubber dinghy to check the strop and buoy. Everything seemed in order, but for the sake of tidiness and good seamanship I decided to trim a few loose strands from around the splice of the strop.

I hauled it across the port tube of the inflatable and with infinite care started to trim the strands with my Stanley knife. It flashed through my mind for a split second that this was rather foolish – then my hand slipped on the slimy rope and the blade made a neat gash in the port tube.

Suddenly, amid a steady whistle of releasing air, I realised my predicament – sitting in a rapidly deflating dinghy in the middle of a fast flowing tidal stream several hundred metres from shore. I found I could stem the flow of air by pressing my wet palm across the gash but, unfortunately, I couldn't reach the outboard starter.

Eventually, I 'took the plunge', so to speak. I released the buoy and mooring, took my hand off the leaking tube, started the motor and headed for the shore at full revs.

Friends watching from the Royal Findhorn Yacht Club veranda told me that it was hilarious to see me heading for the shore at high speed in a banana-shaped inflatable, which ended up folded around me as I stepped gratefully, but with little dignity, on to the beach. • *Joe Leiper*

Foul play!

Nourlangie, a neglected 16 ton Hillyard, came into our lives two years ago, along with a gruelling work regime to restore her to her former glory.

After months of hard work – and with the deadline for Brest 2000 only weeks away – the final task was antifouling. I was fortunate enough to be invited to take part in *Yachting Monthly*'s antifouling test, so, armed with tins of the 'extra-strong' stuff, I set to work.

Nourlangie was sitting on a concrete slipway, which was covered in a few centimetres of mud and, although this hampered work slightly, application was swift. At the end, loaded down with tins and rollers, I started up the stepped sides of the slipway.

My boots, covered in mud, acted like rollerskates and I soon performed an impromptu acrobatic display, ending in a pirouette, a triple salka, a long skid and a backward flip as I fell

with a splatter into the mud, followed closely by a flying tin of antifouling – and its gloopy contents.

The crash and groans of pain alerted my partner, still aboard our yacht. Reaching the deck, she looked below to see an unrecognisable monster – me – covered in foul-smelling mud and antifouling.

As futile attempts were made to clean me up, the phrase 'self-polishing antifouling' took on a new meaning. In the end it was decreed that a visit to the local hospital's accident and emergency department was required.

My arrival was like something out of a horror movie. Children and elderly out-patients ran for cover as The Creature from the Black and Red Lagoon paraded before them. My hopes for sympathy were cruelly dashed as cries of laughter followed. 'Hey! Come and look at this,' they chuckled.

My now glowing body refused to be cleaned by all the lotions and potions available to the nurses. Two broken ribs were diagnosed. Armed with painkillers and a bottle of cleaning agent, I was sent home to have plenty of baths.

'Scrubbing the bottom' also took on a new meaning. Even the bath ended up with a boot-top line. • *Karl Askem*

A dog's life

Our two dogs had progressed with us through various small craft to the Sadler 29, and liked nothing better than a day or two afloat. In those days, we had a drying mooring in Chichester Harbour half a mile down Emsworth Channel, so we had to watch the tides and ferry ourselves and our gear to the boat.

One weekend, we had arranged to meet up with friends at East Head. We left home in good

time but traffic delayed us and we reached Emsworth later than planned. The tide was well in and rising fast. We ran the car down to the landing place and hitched the dogs to a convenient post near the water's edge. Our routine was well practised. The inflatable was too small to carry everything so we used our Mirror dinghy as an additional tender, leaving it on the mooring when we were sailing.

We unloaded the car boot and lifted the Mirror off the roof rack; then the children pumped up the inflatable while I parked the car. Time was getting short. The inflatable was loaded and in the water by the time I returned. We launched the Mirror, clamped on the outboard and tied the inflatable behind. Not a moment to lose. All aboard and off we went.

For once, the outboard started first pull and we had time to relax. 'We might just be in time,' I said, when we were well on our way. 'I hope we haven't forgotten anything.'

My daughter's face dropped. 'The dogs!' she shrieked. 'We've forgotten the dogs!'

Instant panic. We turned and made for the landing place at full throttle. The tide was still rising and we were beside ourselves with worry.

Fortunately we were in time. The dogs were up to their stomachs in the sea, totally unperturbed by their predicament and delighted to see us. But even now, I shudder to think what might have happened. • *Anonymous*

Cap that!

One Saturday morning I left my mooring at Orford in *Heartfelt*, a Westerly Centaur, and headed down the coast towards Harwich Harbour and the Rivers Orwell and Stour. I was singlehanded and hell-bent on testing a new radar I'd fitted that week.

Running alongside the channel and into Harwich Harbour, every ship, every buoy, every yacht showed up on the screen, just where they should be. Even the banks of the river showed up. This was brilliant, I thought, I could even navigate with the radar.

That night I picked up a buoy at Wrabness Cliffs, cooked dinner, enjoyed a good book and went to bed. Next morning dawned dull with rain threatening. I set off up Holbrook Creek to catch the last of the flood up to Mistley and Manningtree, before turning round to carry the ebb all the way back down. This was the plan.

Then Sod's Law sneaked aboard. I was nicely in the channel and could see Stutton Ness beacon about a mile ahead. I could also see a rain squall further ahead.

So, ever safety conscious, I switched on the radar to see how it performed in heavy rain. Radar takes a little time to warm up and then a bit of tuning. So I was head down in the cockpit fiddling with the knobs while the boat was on autopilot.

What, I wondered, is the great black lump on the screen which seems to be directly above me? I looked up to see Stutton Ness beacon, with which we were about to collide. I yanked off the autopilot, pushed the helm hard over and just sneaked past... or so I thought. But a piece of angle iron caught *Heartfelt*'s cap shroud and had us moored to the beacon. The mast was bent double.

The moral of the tale: pay a bit more attention to the scenery and a bit less to the screenery! • *A M Sterling*

Too close for comfort

We looked at each other questioningly. 'Seventy-eight?' The hugely noisy Coastguard helicopter was positioned overhead and the gloved finger of the crewman jabbed again at the blackboard he held. Seventy-eight? Of course. Channel 78.

We had left the Elephant Boat Yard on the Hamble River later than planned, and to reach Chichester Harbour that evening we were motoring into a fresh south-easterly wind.

The sun shone and we watched the great red and white helicopter cruise into view and then position itself almost above a much smaller yacht, a few hundred metres away from our position.

We watched, fascinated, as a line was dropped, taken on board, then followed by a heavier line and a crew member. He

PEYTON

perched in the tiny cockpit, looking like a ton-up motorcyclist who had come to tea and didn't plan to stay long.

While all this was going on, the yacht, which was sailing close-hauled, had come close and we had to veer away.

Subsequently, the whole operation was put into reverse and the crew member was hauled back into the helicopter. It was then that the pilot manoeuvred the helicopter close to us; there was nobody else around.

'Channel 78,' commanded the blackboard. I went below and flicked on the radio, keen to remember the correct routine.

'Did you observe our rescue exercise?' came the question. 'Yes,' I replied, and added that we had found it all very interesting.

Back came the voice of authority: 'You did not keep clear. You put the whole exercise at risk – it could have been a real-life situation.' We motored on our way, feeling rather small.

• *Andrew Black*

Got a light, boy?

Moored comfortably in the sheltered harbour of Richards Bay, South Africa, I staggered out of bed one morning, crawled on deck to turn the gas on and filled the kettle. Flicking the cigarette lighter, the gas burner failed to ignite.

'Damn, the cylinder must be empty!' I thought. I climbed on deck, unscrewed the old cylinder, unlashed the spare from its stowage on the pushpit, connected it up, went down below again and flicked the lighter. Still no flame!

'Hell, there must be a leak somewhere! Quick, turn the gas off sharpish!'

Slightly more awake now, I embarked on a study of the problem. There are three connections between the low pressure side of the regulator and the cooker. What should an intrepid and prudent mariner do? Check each one in turn to find the section with a leak?

Rummaging in the locker for suitable spanners, I disconnected each joint and was rewarded by a satisfying puff from each. I connected them all up again and dribbled detergent on each connection. No sign of a leak. I carefully examined the burners. All okay.

I paused to have a think and rig the windsail to dissipate the gas I'd released. The only idea which presented itself was to have another go with the gas sniffer. (I am fortunate in having a particularly sensitive one, inherited from my father; it's extremely reliable, unless I have a heavy cold.) So I put it to use, sticking my head into every corner of the pipe run. No hint of a leak. By now I was beginning to think I'd imagined the whole thing.

I had another go at lighting the cooker. Grabbed the lighter again and Bingo, it worked! Kettle on, coffee brewing and all was right with the world.

Until lunchtime that is, and blow me if the same thing didn't happen again. Not a flicker from the cooker. Spanners out again and an even more careful examination of the system. Head thrust into some rather damp and nasty corners, no sign of a leak, but this time no miraculous 'light up' either. It looked as though I was going to need Sherlock Holmes to solve the puzzle. Could the regulator have some sort of intermittent blockage, I wondered? Might as well have some lunch and let the left hemisphere of my brain work on the problem. Sometime in mid afternoon, my brain got into gear, fortified perhaps by the can of lager.

'Check the lighter, you idiot!'

I use ordinary gas cigarette lighters, which I buy at the supermarket check-out, usually two or three at a time. Investigation revealed that I had two identical ones (and to add an exotic touch, they bear the legend 'Christmas Island Metro Supermarket Pty Ltd'). And, of course, you will guess that one worked and the other one was as dead as a dodo!

• *John S Newton*

Springing off!

Having made a mess of coming alongside the small boat pontoons just below the upper ferry at Dartmouth three days earlier, I was determined that our departure would be textbook stuff.

With the boat pointing into the tide and no wind, it all seemed to be straightforward. I spent several minutes deciding how to proceed, then explained it all to the crew, who took up their positions. I took off the stern line and forward spring, leaving the bow line (doubled back on board) and the after spring.

It was at this point that my wife, Sue, enquired casually if the inflatable dinghy was tied on. 'Don't worry about the dinghy, it's fine,' I said impatiently.

I gave the signal and my son slipped the bow line; the boat sat back on her spring as planned and the bow moved out gently. Sue engaged forward gear and, as the boat moved off, I slipped the spring and climbed on board at the stern.

The tide now seemed stronger than I'd thought, as we weren't making any headway, so I suggested more power. But by now I had the distinct feeling that we were about to swing right around and berth alongside the yacht behind us.

When I looked back, I realised the importance of Sue's question about the inflatable. Not only had I tied it on the boat; I had also (to prevent its swinging around all night) tied its stern to the pontoon.

By now the dinghy seemed twice as long and half the width that it should have been. With a shout of 'Get it in neutral!' I hung on to the guard wires as we were catapulted backwards at a speed greater than we had ever achieved going forwards. The dinghy proved to be an excellent fender. With the speed of a 100m hurdler I leapt ashore, untied the dinghy and was aboard again before anyone saw us...I think.

We've not been back to that pontoon since. • *Ian McKen*

At full stretch

It had been one of those charters. Having put them ashore, checked the mooring warp and decided the sail covers could wait till morning, I went below for a good tot, a handful of digestive biscuits and oblivion.

Next morning, up early to square the decks, I realised that the young lad who had dropped the main had left the halyard slack. As the yacht had swung in the night, the bight had blown round the spreader and fouled around the steaming light. I should have checked last night.

Luckily, we old-timers know a thing or two. I got out the lead-line, attached the snap shackle on the main halyard to the eye splice on the lead and then slacked away the lead-line while hauling on the halyard.

By now the ebb had begun. As the boat started to swing, the pendular effect aloft increased and the lead swung around the spreader and over the babystay, where it was stuck, as though welded. We had two boathooks, but even when lashed together and held at full stretch while standing on the boom, they were still 6in too short. So I topped up the boom. The early morning ferry slowed alongside and asked how my lead-line had got up there. 'You must have swung it a bit hard!' chortled the skipper.

Meanwhile, ignoring the audience, I continued to wave my 18ft wand as I stood on a slippery sail on an inclined bottom. Eureka, contact! Unfortunately, it was the release ring of the snap shackle. With an unerring aim, the lead-line missile dropped and hit the glass of the forward hatch.

Next time the lead goes aloft, it will most definitely be on a bowline. • *L J Hughes*

Virtual fog

I was undergoing an RYA Yachtmaster examination and having a terrible time. The stress of it all resulted in a complete evaporation of my seagoing abilities and I felt sick, tired and nervous. Only the examiner's vigilance prevented me from piling the nice Westerly Fulmar on to the putty at 6 knots. The combined nudges, hints and meaningful looks from the crew had failed to stop me picking up the man overboard on the wrong side. I was navigating, as it were, in the Last Chance Saloon.

They have this thing called 'blind navigation', otherwise known as 'RYA fog', and I was dreading it. The RYA examiner invited me politely to go into the cabin, whereupon he drew the curtains and said: 'I would like you to imagine that visibility has closed down completely.'

At that very moment, precisely as he uttered those words, visibility in the cabin closed down to zero. There was a giant hissing sound and I could see nothing: not the table, the galley, the charts, nor even the examiner, who had been standing just feet away. My brain, already overloaded, closed down completely and I stared helplessly into the whiteout.

Gradually I made out a pair of eyes peering from where the examiner had been standing. In trying to squeeze between the quarterberth and the chart table my inquisitor had sat on the fire extinguisher, whose safety pin had been removed during an earlier demonstration.

I completed my blind navigation with a fine film of dry powder across the chart and the examiner on the floor with a dustpan and brush. • *Piers Beckett*

The bitter end

It's funny how all our real sailing adventures happened in those early days when we were on a steep learning curve. Our first sailing boat was a *Yachting World* Rambler. We had done some dinghy sailing, and, from a dry mooring on Hayling Island, were beginning to learn the pleasures of cruising.

Navigation was learnt by mistakes. For example, on our first trip to the Isle of Wight we incorrectly identified one of the forts and instead of arriving in Bembridge we found ourselves in Seaview.

The first time we anchored under sail at East Head, I headed into wind and screamed at Liz, my wife, to drop the mainsail and let go the anchor.

'How much warp do you want out, darling?' called my loving wife.

'Just let the whole bloody warp out and get that mainsail down on to the boom, but *be quick!*' I screamed back.

She did, then returned to the cockpit and made her skipper a cup of tea.

I was sipping contentedly when I noticed a piece of rope floating in the water not far from us. Then I remarked that all the other boats seemed to be dragging their anchors. God, no, it was us!

Liz ran forward. We were not attached to our anchor. There was no warp left. We were drifting quickly now and started to yell as we approached another cruiser. The owner came out of the cabin and went to fend us off just where Liz was standing. He had both his hands on her breasts as the owner's wife emerged from the cabin!

I now know the meaning of the 'bitter end', and one of the first jobs I do on each new boat is to make sure the anchor warp is firmly attached inside the anchor locker. • *Mike Morris*

Sailing by ear!

It was a beautiful night in mid Atlantic. The mate was asleep below and I had the watch. We were motor-sailing in light winds and, with little to do, I decided to catch up on the laundry.

The clothes I was wearing being ripe, I stripped off and added them to the bucket. Initially the wind deserted us and the genoa began to flog, so I furled it and we motored on under main alone. The sail rolled up nicely but I could see by torchlight that there was something not right with the clew, so

torch in hand I walked up to the foredeck.

Looking up I could see a patch of torn sail. To reach it I had to go on tiptoe, where I could just poke at it with the torch. It was now, with my head hard against the sail, that the barb on my earring twisted itself into the lay of the genoa sheet.

What had seemed a gentle sea from the cockpit was not so benign as I now swung around by my ear. The boat was lifting to the swell about a metre, and when she came down I had to bend my knees to stay balanced, which put my whole weight on my ear. My ear began to stretch. Unwrapping my arms from around the furled sail, to which I was now clinging like a limpet, immediately added another inch. Being clipped on is one thing but being clipped on by the head is something different altogether.

Decision time: I could lose part of my ear, or I could wait for the mate to come up and find me there, swinging naked by my lug. No question about it, the ear had to go!

The boat went up, I came down, someone screamed, then the ring straightened out and I dropped free. I made it back to the cockpit just as the mate came up and asked: 'Quiet watch?'

'Yes,' I replied. 'I spent some time hanging around on the foredeck.' • *Gary E Brown*

Up the pole

The sea was a picture of tranquillity – white-laced wavelets rolled effortlessly towards a hazy horizon, while the sun dazzled in reflective brilliance. It was a perfect day for my first singlehanded race in *Clairella*. And I couldn't have made a better start – first over the line and well upwind of the man to beat.

A close fetch in a force 2 took us from Cowes towards the Nab Tower. Passing the Forts, we realised that half the fleet had given up on the failing breeze. Some six hours later we were still wallowing short of the Nab Tower when frustration got the better of the other four skippers. Shortly after, I threw in the towel too, the last to retire and a moral victory achieved.

I put on the autopilot for the 15-mile run back to Warsash while I tidied up the boat. It was dusk now, nav lights on. However, the steaming light refused to provide any illumination. Flat calm, flat sea and not another vessel in sight. With mast steps, changing the bulb should be a simple, safe one-man job, so 8m above deck, facing aft, I wrapped an arm around the mast ready to disassemble the light.

Tiring from the awkward position, I took a rest. Suddenly, in my peripheral vision I glimpsed a wave, a rather big wave. It was dead ahead, approaching at about 10 knots and concealing the black bows of a 200 ton barge. O Lord!

There wasn't time to climb down the mast and get to the helm before collision time. But was he really coming straight for me? I spotted a minor asymmetry in his profile and hoped for the best. Within seconds he was abreast of me. I clung frantically to the lower mast as his wash hit me and the great black monster slid past – all of 9m to port. His unlit wheelhouse was silent and empty. Perhaps he was looking for a spare light bulb.

• *Neil Millward*

Link call laughter

We were taking part in the Round The Island Race and the wind had deserted us. We were all bunched up off Bembridge Ledge, getting pretty fed up as it was hot and we all knew we would miss the last of the tide to the finish.

From out in the fleet, someone put in a link call. I confess I tuned in to listen and I'm sure many other boats switched on the VHF too. It went like this:

'Hello, Mary, John here. Over.'

'Hello, darling, where are you? Over.'

'We're all off Bembridge Ledge, there's no wind. Over.'

'Not to worry, darling. I'll put a nice roast on. Over.'

'We'll be a little late, Mary, but that'll be nice. What roast will it be? Over.'

'I thought I would do lamb. Over.'

'Great, Mary – will that be leg? Over.'

Sorry, I didn't hear any more as my crew collapsed in laughter. • *Peter Nuttycombe*

African Queen, Solent-style

Tidal calculations were never my strong point. That's why I bought a Southerly lifting keel yacht. But it still looked promising as we anchored in Newtown Creek, on the Isle of Wight. An eternal optimist, I insisted we could make it by dinghy to the jetty landing, halfway to the New Inn, before it was as dry as our throats.

At first all went well – dinghy inflated, outboard started first pull, and John and I, plus wives and my 10-year-old son, motored upstream.

I was concerned that full throttle was giving only stately progress, but surely this was because of the load, not the strength of the current? The jetty was round two more bends and, although the channel was narrowing, I was sure we could make it past the immaculate, pastel-clad couple in the dinghy ahead.

It was then that the prop bit solidly into the mud, almost throwing John over the bow. With the outboard at shallow setting, we proceeded another 20 yards before grounding again. John unshipped the oars but had to admit that rowing through mud was not getting us anywhere.

Shoes, socks off, jeans off, I leapt over the side with unwise gusto to find that, whilst the water was merely ankle deep, the underlying goo stopped above my knees. As I put the painter over my shoulder and leant into it Bogart *African Queen*-style, I could see the pastel plastic paddlers gaining steadily.

Once I had the knack of balancing in the ooze, pulling the dinghy was surprisingly easy over wet mud, and over the next 100 yards I opened a healthy lead over the pastel crew. As our dinghy touched bottom, John disrobed and slid over the side.

Our wives exchanged concerned glances after comparing the dregs of the ebb under us to the remaining 150 yards to dry land. They were surprisingly compliant when I suggested they join us in the mud, tucking dresses into knickers and reminding me strangely of childhood playgrounds. Think leeches, mangroves, Katharine Hepburn and rapids. Sandra (mine) wore a condescending 'here we go again' expression. Vesna (John's) muttered in her mother tongue of the beneficial effects of mud on the complexion.

Son Mark, now the only dinghy occupant, reclined in splendour. Sandra and Vesna plodded precariously through the mud, steadying themselves on the dinghy tubes. John and I, after several moments of imbalance and abortive attempts at remaining vertical, were now past caring.

We reached the jetty and made it to the pub with plenty of bar time and even for last food orders. The pastel crew arrived later in pristine condition, just as 'Time, gentlemen' was about to be called. • *Raymond Prowse*

Nuits St Georges

Years ago, before the advent of its marina, Porquerolles Harbour, on the island of that name east of Toulon, was a pleasant haven for the few who knew of it. At anchor there one July evening in the 17.7m (58ft) ketch *Minots Light* we then owned, my wife Germaine and I watched a newly arrived sloop anchor and drag.

It was getting dark and from enlightened self-interest we invited the sloop, called *Nuits St Georges*, to tie alongside for the night. Asked about the name, the young skipper told us that his father, the owner, was a *négociant* in Burgundy who specialised in wine from this region. He then presented us with three unlabelled bottles of 'wine too good to sell'. In the morning he left and we continued our cruise along the coast. The wine turned out to be superb, among the very best we'd ever had.

A month later *Minots Light* was anchored in Port Man on the island of Port Cros. Although Port Man is as notable for poor holding as for natural beauty, we hoped for a few tranquil days. Alas, a north-easterly squall whooshed in and everybody began to drag. As Germaine struggled to evade out-of-control boats

while I got the anchor up, a sloop came perilously close. Her skipper shouted to me what sounded like 'How do you like the wind?' I gave him a few apt adjectives as he swept past. Then I saw the sloop's name, *Nuits St Georges*.

He had been asking about his *vin* (pronounced approximately 'van') which I had misheard as *vent* (approximately 'von'). We never saw *Nuits St Georges* again and remain mortified to this day. • *Arthur Beiser*

The big blockage

We had almost finished a world circumnavigation when the forward heads became blocked. Who should tell the skipper? 'Don't shoot the messenger,' I begged him. 'The loo's blocked up!' He was not amused.

'What have you put down that you haven't eaten?' he queried sternly.

'Not guilty, sir!' came the timid response, but of course he didn't believe me. Grimly, skipper rolled up his sleeves and began to dismantle pipes, valves and pump. An ominous silence hung heavily over the boat and his usual 'whistle while he worked' was noticeably absent. Only the occasional gurgle and glug broke the silence, indicating progress.

Suddenly, bursting from the heads, he rushed through the saloon, bucket in hand. Systematically the parts were washed and examined on deck, then I heard a chuckle, 'Well I'll be damned, you'll never believe this, Inga!'

Between finger and thumb he was holding an elephant – a very tiny wooden elephant, about 2cm square. It was one of four which had been given to us in Sri Lanka, but which had subsequently gone missing soon after we left Port Said. Her bid for freedom had almost succeeded.

'Ellie' had passed through the inlet valve, staying in the pump for over a month before sticking in the outlet valve. But the question, 'How did she get there?' remained unanswered until another elephant made a bid for freedom in rough seas off Crete and was discovered hiding behind a cushion.

We concluded that the 'loo blocker' had probably fallen into the nightshirt of female crew asleep in the port bunk and been inadvertently transported to the heads. • *Inga Chapman*

Inflammable inflatable

Is the maiden trip of the yachting season akin to the first rugby game of the year when, statistically, most injuries occur?

I was motoring my Falmouth Gypsy 24-footer (7m), singlehanded, from her winter lay-up at the boatyard to her mooring, near Dittisham, and the Dart.

The gods clearly were trying to tell me something when, on arrival, I found my mooring occupied by another vessel. On picking up an adjacent buoy, my spectacles fell off and slid gently below the surface, to disappear for ever.

After tidying and locking *Naiad*, I jumped into my loaded inflatable to motor to Greenway Quay, half a mile downriver.

Warning number three was issued from above, when my year-old outboard refused to start. After many attempts, each making me less capable of reason, I decided to check the petrol level. This is not quite as easy as it sounds, as my inflatable is small; positioning oneself above the filler orifice to obtain a good view takes the stern down below water level. In order to look down the filler opening, I pulled the outboard back on its tilt mechanism. This immediately disproved the theory of an empty tank, as petrol cascaded out of it. As complete rage took over, I made a final attempt to start my hated motor. With a gentle whoomph, the spilt fuel ignited.

Being beyond the years of gymnastic ability, I surprised myself at the speed with which I returned to mother vessel. As I fumbled with the many similar keys to open the hatch and grab the fire extinguisher, my imagination was computing the effect of the explosion of an almost full tank of petrol and burning inflatable rubber on *Naiad*'s GRP hull and wooden upperworks.

The gods, however, decided that enough was enough, the conflagration retreating rapidly under the onslaught of the extinguisher.

As I rowed back to the quay, the cause of my problems became obvious. I had failed to replace the plug lead after winter storage. • *Steve Jones*

Wheel deal

Despite our limited knowledge and experience, my wife and I purchased our first boat, a 12.8m (42ft) Moody, and had it berthed in Ibiza. We thought we would learn the best way, hands on, bit by bit.

The first evening, after dinner, was spent sipping wine in the cockpit and talking about the new life ahead of us whilst in awe at the beauty of the stars overhead. But the frustration of the wheel! It kept spinning round every time I put my feet on it.

'Ahah! That's what the tightening knob is for,' I deduced. The wheel stopped spinning and I could then relax with my feet up. Next morning adventures beckoned, and my wife, with even less experience than myself, took the wheel. We were bows-to the pontoon and, as we reversed out, the propeller kick turned us so that we were leaving the marina backwards.

'She won't steer,' said my wife, with some concern. 'No problem,' I said, talking with the undeserved confidence of an old sea dog. 'She needs speed before she will start steering properly. Be brave, more throttle.' But she still wouldn't steer, and I couldn't believe it. I had just discovered that my wife was totally incompetent and couldn't even steer a boat!

As we hurtled backwards at 5 knots I thought of swapping the boat for a villa, when I suddenly became distracted by the bow of a sleek and shiny Sunseeker over my shoulder. It was the last boat parked on the pontoon before the open sea. Crunch – straight into his anchor, buckling our back rail and smashing our nice new outboard.

We are getting more proficient now, although my wife has decided to learn without my assistance! I also have this strange, unusual habit of checking the wheel knob before we set forth anywhere. • *David Bennett*

A free ride

Heading downwind toward the dock at the end of an excellent, blustery day's sailing, I felt a well-executed landing under sail would finish things off nicely.

I had sailed my swing-keel Catalina 22 on and off this floating pontoon, which serves as a public dock, umpteen times over the years in all sorts of conditions. Old hat.

John was below, cranking up the keel as depths shoal right by the dock. Once he had done that, he would place himself on the port sidedeck with a midships spring, ready to step off by a specific cleat on the dock, and bring us to a stop alongside. Fenders were out and jib sheets let go. The wind was blowing perpendicular to the dock so, seconds out, as I started the starboard turn, I left the main well out to port, soon to lose power.

The following happened in about seven seconds:

A lady holidaymaker emerged from a tour launch on the other side of the dock, clutching her sunhat to her head against the breeze. A shoulder bag was slung across her chest. She gesticulated to John that she would take his rope.

We were now 2ft from the dock, not yet fully turned – and moving. As I replied to John's enquiring look: 'No, definitely not', the other half of my brain was much more concerned with the grievous bodily harm I was about to inflict on this lady with the boom, which was now sweeping the width of the dock.

All I could do was to haul in on the mainsheet at panic speed, which effected rapid acceleration and, especially with the keel up and John on the lee sidedeck, a really horrendous broach against the dock. The next thing I knew, I was passing John, who was a heap on the dock and, looking forward, saw that the flailing jib sheet had snagged this woman's shoulder-bag, and was whisking her along the dock, the end of which was a rapidly diminishing 12ft away.

I was reminded of a person chasing down a railway platform whilst clinging to the end of the fast-departing last train home – which inspired me to leap from tiller to sidedeck and haul this poor soul aboard.

We were off the dock immediately, broaching wildly, but I found myself wondering, even as I untangled her and introduced myself, whether I would be sentenced for attempted handbag snatching or kidnapping. • *Hamish Tear*

Pull of the sea

To show that we didn't care that our girlfriends didn't want to go to the College Ball, we had hired a boat on the Broads. We were moored to a wooden jetty in a narrow creek facing away from the open water. It was a beautiful morning when I awoke at 0500 but my three colleagues slept soundly. Pulling a sweater over my pyjamas, I crept out into the cockpit. At 0600 they still slept, but I could stand inactivity no longer.

All this was in the days before boats had engines. But I had read my sailing instruction book. The wind was light, so I hoisted the gaff mainsail and the jib. Still they slept. I cast off the bow rope and allowed the boat to turn gently round to face the river. Still they slept.

On the jetty, I took the stern rope in my hand ready to let go. It was then that I realised a boat under full sail pulled harder than I could. The gap was already too wide to get back aboard. Split-second decision: let my friends go, or jump. Still holding the rope, I jumped. As we sailed out into the open broad, three tousled heads appeared over the stern, apparently finding the sight of a singlehanded sailor being towed behind in his pyjamas highly amusing. • *Brendan Sewill*

Anchor buoy dance

All experienced skippers know how to look foolish with great authority. I conned our Fisher 30, *Kyle Rhea*, into Alicante harbour. Maureen hooked the visitors' buoy. With the tender now inflated and shoreside restaurants exuding the compelling aroma of Mediterranean olive oil, garlic and charcoal, there remained the simple task of checking the mooring.

I discovered that the visitors' buoy carried a great deal of scope. I realised that it actually held a bow rope from which you could go 'stern-to' the jetty.

I am always doubtful about the holding power of this system and only trust any ground tackle after careful tests. I pulled the mooring very hard.

It was about this time that one of the yacht shore parties, vibrating to the throb of Alicante, came to my notice. Deck dancing is uncommon in my experience, so I paused to think and observe the animated figures.

I thought that either they were dancing manically to Queen's *We Will Rock You*, or something was amiss. At first it seemed quite reasonable that, with limited deck space for fancy footwork, arm swinging was a feature of free expression.

However, I soon came to realise that there were no visitors' buoys in Alicante; no fixed ground tackle, only occasional anchor buoys, placed by a conscientious skipper. Oops!

Sorry, fellow mariner! We all make mistakes and, thankfully, I couldn't trip your anchor. My own anchor buoy is now marked with a skull and crossbones. • *Peter Dronfield*

At the sharp end

Following an 18 month refit of my Rival 32, *Ayton Serenade*, I took her out for sea trials on a February day with my friend, Mike. By the time we returned, the wind had risen considerably and I was pleased to see my wife Barbara on the lock pontoon waiting to take our lines.

Leaving the lock, we decided that on arrival at our berthing pontoon, Mike would leap ashore, and Barbara, dressed in a tight-fitting pencil skirt and ill-prepared for leaping anywhere, would stand at the bow and take the line from Mike.

Mike leapt heroically onto the pontoon and then the wind gusted, blowing us across it. I slammed the engine into reverse, gave it full throttle and pulled away from the pontoon into the middle of the marina basin.

After straightening up, I motored around in a large circle to make another approach. But Mike was nowhere to be seen. I was just thinking how inconsiderate it was of him to disappear

PEYTON

when I noticed Barbara's skirt was split from hem to waistline and showing a good deal more of her than was healthy in February. It also struck me as odd that, for a woman not generally given to acts of flagrant exhibitionism, she was doing nothing to cover herself up. Indeed, she was apparently totally occupied with some aspect of the stemhead fitting.

It was then that I noticed a pair of white knuckles on each side of the bow roller. The knuckles then sprouted a face, a very red face with bulging eyes. Then a leg appeared aboard, and slowly Barbara heaved an exhausted Mike on deck.

As I'd slammed the boat into reverse Mike had been at full stretch with feet on the pontoon and both hands on the bow. With the strength of purpose born of impending doom, he pulled himself up under the anchor, sure that I was aware of his plight. But I wasn't. And Barbara, having caught her arm in his lifejacket harness, couldn't tell me. She told me all about it later, though! • *Brian S Ferguson*

Rude awakening

The skipper promised a pleasant weekend, and we set off from Gosport in *Ginger*, our varnished Folkboat, to sail on the tide in warm and calm conditions to Studland Bay.

My new hairdo stayed in place and we arrived sedately, dropped anchor and opened a bottle of wine as we surveyed Old Harry and Ballard Down in the sunset.

As night fell, the wind shifted and increased considerably. *Ginger* began to pitch and toss at her anchor and waves came rolling in from seaward. We decided we'd turn in. I wrapped my glamorous long nightie carefully about my legs as I climbed into my sleeping bag and I fell asleep.

We were rudely awoken by a loud yell from a neighbouring boat '*Ginger*, you're dragging!'

The skipper commanded, 'Out! No time to dress. Get the anchor up now!'

I rushed forward with swirling pink froth about my legs, just as the frantic skipper switched on the deck-light.

A huge gust of wind snatched at my nightie which, anchored only by the arms, did its level best to take off. Still the deep voice boomed over the deck, '*Hurry up!*'

Nowadays I make sure I always wear pyjamas on board.

• *Margaret Smith*

Jetsam revisited

This is a story of rare chance – not the common chance that afflicts us all, where happily disposable boat kit on its way overboard lodges precariously on a stanchion or rigging awaiting recovery, whereas more valuable items slip effortlessly into the sea.

Merioneth Yacht Club has an annual race, a return trip from Barmouth around Bardsey Island on the north-west extremity of Wales. It's known as the 20,000 Saints Race.

My wife Jill and I set off on the race, which started at midnight. Being her first sail of the season and a rough sea, Jill was soon affected by *mal-de-mer* and took to her bunk with a washing-up bowl. Off Abersoch we decided to abandon the race

PEYTON

and, against all the ecological rules, but to improve the environment on the boat, we committed the washing-up bowl to the deep.

Six weeks later we were on passage from the Isle of Man to Holyhead, returning from Port William after the Three Peaks Yacht Race.

We were sailing briskly on a close reach in the choppy tidal waters off Anglesey with evening setting in. It was only the second time in three years that we had sailed these waters. Well heeled and facing the bright sea, an object, half submerged and upturned, flashed before our eyes.

Fish storage box, I thought; Jill thought it was a large luncheon box. Then the truth dawned. In unison we exclaimed complete recognition of our discarded washing-up bowl. It had drifted some 50 miles from where it had been jettisoned. Passed in a trice there was no time to grab it and it was not valuable enough to initiate a man-overboard drill.

The mind boggles at the infinite chance that we should see it again, such that we are looking forward to winning the National Lottery at much shorter odds. • *Ian Hudson*

Yellow peril

It was our summer cruise and we had chartered a yacht from Mylor to explore the Devon coast. The crew were due to arrive on Friday evening – Jude, as usual, last of all. As her ETA was around midnight, she asked me to fly something from the shrouds to let her know which boat was ours.

Just before midnight, and with the Scotch bottle on the ebb, Jude arrived, having spotted the flag illuminated by the decklight. Five minutes later came a knocking on the hull. I went on deck to find a large RIB alongside containing three Customs officers.

'Where from?' they inquired, in time-honoured fashion.

'London,' I replied, adding, 'by car, today.' Then the awful realisation set in.

I'd chosen the flag most likely to be seen at a distance, but without thinking of its true purpose. It had seemed quite proper to fly the vibrantly yellow Q flag as a signal for Jude.

After hearing my shamefaced explanation and radioing to cancel their rummage team from Exeter, the Customs officers were quite understanding.

Two days later we were enjoying the sun and pasties in Fowey when we read in the local paper that on the same night Customs officers had raided a yacht in the Helford River and found heroin with a street value of over £1 million. Somehow I don't think they were flying the yellow jack. • *Gordon Cobban*

Doorstop technique

I felt I could sail singlehanded anywhere in my little gaff cutter, *Chough*. She was just 5.8m (19ft) on the deck with a 1.8m (6ft) bowsprit and no engine. We had an inside trot on the north-to-south pile moorings on the Medina at Cowes.

To sail on to the mooring I had a gusty south-westerly breeze. The distance between each line of piles was barely 15.2m (50ft). I thought better of the windward approach and opted for the downwind, semi-suicidal option.

I thought I had enough power to round up through 180° and make directly for the mooring.

I lowered the foresails upwind, judged the moment, swung round hard to port and expected to slide up on to my mooring, head to wind. It was then that I realised there was a good ebb running. I was unable to round up in time without hitting the wooden motor yacht just downstream of my mooring. It was inevitable that I'd hit her, but I didn't want to spoil our topsides.

In a moment of inspiration, I noticed she had high bulwarks and, midway along, there was a removable door. I aimed for this at speed with my bowsprit and pierced it expertly. This broke our speed and our hulls never touched. I pulled myself up to my mooring and removed the door from the end of the bowsprit.

I made a new door for the motor yacht, screwed on the original capping, painted it and fitted it the next day. I don't think the owner ever knew! • *Robert Cundall*

Hungry hamster

My daughter's trembling bottom lip said it all...the hamster had to come too. And so Truffles, complete with cage, sawdust, food and sundry toys to keep her mind off seasickness, was loaded aboard our Westerly, together with everything a family needs for a week's cruise.

Our bilge-keeler settled peacefully on the sand in Ilfracombe Harbour and we set about enjoying all the delights of this Victorian seaside town. We were surprised at how well the hamster had fitted in and impressed with her ability to be self-gimballing, hanging from the top of her cage. We even made her our honorary Ship's Rat.

I was to look after Truffles in the cockpit, while my daughter, Jenny, washed the cage below.

I decided to let Truffles play among the coils of reefing lines that lie untidily either side of the companionway. Scurrying over this exciting new territory, she made a sudden dash for freedom into a hole in the coaming.

I remained calm for a few seconds and tried to entice her back, but both children spotted what had happened and started to cry.

They placed tasty treats at every hamster-sized hole along the coachroof, but it became increasingly clear that Truffles had managed to find the only truly inaccessible area to finish her cruise.

Even my husband, a normally placid man, seemed unable to finish a sentence; 'How could you. . . ?', 'Why didn't you. . . ?' etc. I was nearly in tears too, when we heard the unmistakable sound of gnawing from behind the instrument panel. My husband leapt below and returned, brandishing a screwdriver while we stood by, waiting to grab anything that moved.

The instrument panel was unscrewed frantically and gently prised out. Behind, sat a perfectly contented hamster, surrounded by tiny chewed fragments, clutching our transducer cable in her mouth. • *Amanda Ivey*

Heads and tales

I was helping a friend of mine, Nick, to prepare for a three-month trip to the Med. He was up to his elbows in the engine, rebuilding the cylinder head. It never was a very good starter. Nick asked me to remove the toilet pump. Charming job, I thought. But if it helps I'd be delighted to do it.

'Here's a bucket for any residual water left in the pipes,' said Nick. Ever keen to do a good job I was paranoid about making a mess. I closed the seacocks and checked to make sure they were closed. I inched each pipe off the pump and quickly placed it over the bucket. Perfect! Only a few drops spilled on the sole.

I then removed the pump and put it in my bag to clean it up and replace all the seals at home. As ever, always eager to impress, I started to clean the heads area, picking up all the tools and mopping up the spilled water with a sponge and squeezing it into the now nearly full bucket of water. Spotless! I then emptied the bucket into the toilet. • *Jim Abbey*

Lift and separate

After being involved in the superyacht world, I decided to go back to my roots and buy an old Mirror dinghy to do up during the winter. The day came to launch *Min* (throwback from *The Goons* radio programme). She looked spick and span, with gleaming white paintwork and glossy varnished woodwork. A sail down the River Hamble and over to Ashlett Creek seemed a good idea.

We zig-zagged our way to Ashlett jetty on a hot Sunday morning and tied up comfortably. We were the only boat there. After going for a long walk wearing bikini and shorts, I came back to the pub, where a Sunday crowd was gathered with nothing much to do but sit and stare. By now, *Min* was hemmed in by a clutter of sailing school dinghies and worse, the tide had gone out and the outboard was jammed under another boat. As I sat in the dinghy, my crew spent about ten minutes upside down at the stern trying to extricate the engine.

I asked a man on the quay to pass down the painter and held up my arm. Ping, and my bikini top popped off! I hastily covered myself in confusion and asked him to 'wait one second' while I retrieved my top and dignity. Again, I asked for the painter and moved forward, only to find that I could not move. I'd done up my bra around the stay. By now I was laughing nervously – and yet again asked for the painter. Not once did the man smile or move a muscle, which didn't help.

We finally left the quay, much to the amusement of the Sunday clientele from the pub and my companion said: 'You were not much help to me with the engine!' I had to admit that I had my own problems up front! • *Diana Jung*

These fuelish things

We'd been sailing in Spanish waters for just over a month; both the Atlantic and now the Mediterranean. My husband, Dave, had spent a couple of months before our departure learning Spanish from cassette tapes. He'd picked up the lingo very well and I was quietly impressed.

Gasalina is Spanish for petrol and *gasoleo* is what is used for diesel. Two very similar words, as I'm sure most will appreciate.

One thing we quickly learned about the Med is that there is either no wind or too much. The 'too much' comes in the form of levanters, tramontanas, mistrals and vendavales etc. With no wind, we were motoring around and using more fuel than initially anticipated.

At Fuengirola, we pulled up to the fuel dock. The attendant shouted '*Gas*****?*'

We had a yacht, so what else would we want!

I inserted the fuel pump nozzle, while Dave was below checking the level in the tank. While I was squatting there, it did cross my mind that the pipe had a red handle, and in England red is for petrol and blue or black is for diesel. I didn't think any more of it, confident that my husband and the attendant must know what they were doing.

When the tank was full, Dave went to pay and it was not until he saw the attendant replace the fuel pipe that he saw to his horror we'd topped our diesel tank up with petrol.

He explained to the attendant, who didn't seem fazed. He just went and rounded up numerous containers. Dave and he spent the next three hours hand pumping the 100 litre tank dry. It was sweltering below deck and each time one of them came up after a shift they were drenched in perspiration. I was happy to be left out of it.

When the tank was empty it was refilled with the right *gasoleo* – diesel.

The finishing blow was that we had to pay for both the petrol and diesel.

An expensive and time-consuming mistake. After that experience, Dave always made a point about double checking his hearing for the words *gasalina* and *gasoleo*.

• *Deborah Christiansen-Lee*

Ah, the trials of youth!

Several years ago, being the novice member of an inexperienced crew of three, we were on holiday on the Norfolk Broads in a small sailing vessel with little headroom and even less room in the heads.

As an introduction to a sea toilet, instructions were given explaining the mechanism, intricacies and workings of this wondrous contraption. Came the eventful moment when I had to 'go', I squeezed into the compartment and closed the door. A short while later, having managed the almost impossible task of turning round, I pumped. The pressure was building up nicely so I continued pumping. I stopped, realising that all was not well. I began to wish that I had been a little more attentive during the explanation.

Uneasily, I attended to one seacock and then the other, adjusting the position of each. I pumped again. I knew that things didn't feel quite right but I was not sure and, being a callow youth, didn't want to ask. I pumped again. I adjusted the seacocks once more but the pressure in the system remained. I pumped again to the point where the solid feel of the now immovable pump handle began to concern me.

Inevitably there was a fizzy, squelchy bang and the jubilee clip holding the outlet pipe to the pump gave up the unequal struggle. I spent a long time cleaning, washing, showering, replacing the hose and apologising.• *Alan Otterburn*

Laid up legless

Elizabeth Mary has spent a good part of her 75 years on legs,
the first 30 working out of Polperro, that delightful little drying
harbour in South Cornwall. Lately, laying up on the beach with
her new set of legs has proved the old fisherman's wisdom – it
is cheap and keeps her wet: two vital factors in keeping a small
part of Britain's maritime history sailing.

One October Sunday, the late afternoon tide was right for
laying-up, with a fair wind up the creek to the beach. *Elizabeth
Mary* has no engine; that adds to the excitement of sailing the
river with her 26ft increased by 14ft of bowsprit. The crew's
anxiety evaporated visibly as we tacked gently upriver, dodging
through the trots of moored craft, cannily using the flood to
drift us past all those plastic sterns. A hint of superiority could
perhaps have been read on our faces as we bore away into the
creek. We enjoyed the sensuous pleasure of sailing where others
would motor; we took pride in maintaining that tradition of
ship-handling embodied by her first fisherman owner.

The wind died as we ghosted past the massive oaks,
following the narrow, winding channel. We gybed within 10
yards of the dam and the light was fading as we sailed on to the
beach; a fitting end to a great season.

I sculled my crew ashore and returned in the dark to put out
anchors and lines. The tide rose a few more inches. I made some

adjustments to the warps and, at last satisfied that *Elizabeth Mary* was in the right place for the winter, drove home, enjoying a glow of achievement instead of that last cool mental check.

'How did it go? Did you remember to put the nuts on the leg bolts?' asked my wife. A long and deflating pause. The kitchen clock showed it would be high water. I had just 20 minutes to get back to the boat, extract the legs from under the cockpit sole and bolt them on. • *Julian Burn*

Bucket and don't chuck-it

I use a two-bucket system when sailing long distance: yellow for salt water and cooking and blue for bilge water and anything else mucky.

It was dark, wet and windy. The Monitor windvane was not working properly and I went on deck to adjust it, stumbling over both buckets in the cockpit. Annoyed, I chucked the blue bucket below and switched over from the windvane to the electronic autopilot. Back below, coffee and warmth beckoning, I slipped on the blue bucket and chucked it back in the cockpit.

Just about to get out of my waterproofs for the first time that day, the boat suddenly swung wildly into the wind. Stopping only to grab a torch, I went back up into the cockpit. The Autohelm steering arm had come adrift from the tiller. Why? Because the blue bucket had rolled down the cockpit and jammed between the seat and tiller.

Thus one Autohelm arm, working impeccably, was now stuck on top of a blue bucket and not connected. The problem remedied, I stepped back to go down below and put my foot in the yellow bucket – full of water. • *Peter Crowther*

Creature from the deep

Spring 1981 was a period of intense excitement in the household as launch time approached. We had completed the fitting out of our new Westerly GK24 *Pacer* during an intense winter's work and looked forward to the rewards of our labours.

High tide was around midnight and I calculated that there should be enough water to float her off her trailer around 2330. It was a perfect night with not a ripple on the water as darkness fell and I waited with my 14-year-old daughter for the moment the yacht floated for the first time.

By 2315 the magic moment arrived and with a couple of bumps she was off. Like all East Coast estuaries, our moorings are of necessity well offshore and I started the Vire inboard engine with not a little trepidation. It was my first attempt at installing an engine and I had doubts about the folding prop.

My worst fears were soon realised. The engine refused to drive the boat at more than one knot. We made it to our mooring as the ebb was beginning to run strongly.

My second worry was whether the boat would float to her marks. I decided to check with the torch. Leaning over the side I almost jumped back in fright. Under the boat was the outline of a large creature in the water. My road trailer was still hanging firmly from the keel!

Sunday was spent recovering the trailer with the help of friends and some oil drums and at the expense of a few ribald comments about 'Trailer Sailors'. Without the trailer, the engine drove *Pacer* perfectly! • *George H Shields*

Bare-faced cheek

It was the summer of 1950 and my engineless Montague whaler was anchored in Largs Bay on the Firth of Clyde. In those days there were rowing boats for hire all round the Clyde area and, as we didn't have our own dinghy, it was normal to get a lift ashore and back from one of the lads in a rowing boat. However on this occasion, having got a lift ashore, my crew and I lingered there too long and when we returned to the quay all the rowing boats were locked up for the night. We were stranded.

We had three choices: go to a hotel (too expensive); sleep in a promenade shelter (too uncomfortable), or borrow a dinghy from the stone pier.

We decided on the last option and borrowed a clinker dinghy. Back on the whaler we tied it to the stern, took the oars on board, and settled down for the night. However, just before dawn, I noticed the dinghy was missing. It had not been tied up properly and was bumping gently on the pebble beach 122m away.

I asked my crew to swim after it, but he declined. There was no alternative. I had to swim after it myself. I took off all my clothes and, with an oar on each arm, swam ashore.

Eventually my knees touched the beach, but as I stood up with an oar in each hand and no clothes on, I noticed an old lady gathering driftwood. When she noticed me, she ran off the beach screaming.

She must have thought it was another Viking raid.

• *Roger K Steele*